CLEVELAND BUILDS AN ART MUSEUM

PATRONAGE, POLITICS, AND ARCHITECTURE 1884-1916

OCT. 22, 1914

Frontispiece. South portico (main entrance) of The Cleveland Museum of Art under construction, October 1914. The use of monolithic column shafts over 24 feet long ensured consistent tapering of the column's diameter and uninterrupted fluting. The results communicate both strength and grace.

CLEVELAND BUILDS AN ART MUSEUM

PATRONAGE, POLITICS, AND ARCHITECTURE 1884-1916

WALTER C. LEEDY, JR.

Published by The Cleveland Museum of Art
1991

This publication was underwritten by a generous grant from the Horace Kelley Art Foundation.

Library of Congress Cataloging-in-Publication Data
Leedy, Walter C.
    Cleveland builds an art museum: patronage, politics, and architecture, 1884-1916 / Walter C. Leedy, Jr.
        p.   cm.
    Includes bibliographical references and index.
    ISBN 0-940717-09-3
    1. Cleveland Museum of Art. I. Title.
N552.L44 1991
708.171'32—dc20   91-3424
                                          CIP

Editors: Jo Zuppan and Rachel G. Feingold
Designer: Thomas H. Barnard III
Production Coordinator: Emily S. Rosen
Printed by Eastern Press, New Haven, Connecticut

Photo credits: Frontispiece, Figs. 7-9, 11, 13-14, 17-18, 19 [Building Committee Minutes, July 3, 1911], 20-25, 29, 31, 33-37, 41, 45, 47, 49, 57-59, Archives, The Cleveland Museum of Art; Figs. 1, 12, 15, 46, courtesy of the Western Reserve Historical Society; Fig. 2, after *Atlas of Cuyahoga County, Ohio* (Philadelphia, 1874), details, pp. 76-77; Fig. 3, after Geo. C. F. Cram, J. H. Beers, and J. Q. A. Bennett, *Atlas of Cuyahoga County and the City of Cleveland, Ohio: Official Maps and Records* (Chicago, 1892), pt. 20; Fig. 4, courtesy of Case Western Reserve University Archives; Fig. 5, 52, courtesy of Cleveland Public Library, Photograph Collection; Fig. 6, courtesy Buffalo and Erie County Historical Society; Fig. 10, after *Plat-Book of the City of Cleveland and Suburbs*, 2 vols. (Philadelphia, 1912), 1: details of pls. 17, 35; Fig. 16, *Cleveland Plain Dealer*, January 17, 1909; Figs. 26-28, 32, 38-39, 43-44, 50-51, 53-54, 56, courtesy of Registrar's Office, The Cleveland Museum of Art; Fig. 30, after *Architectural Record* 40, 3 (1916): 198; Figs. 40, 48, courtesy of *The Cleveland Press* Collection, The Cleveland State University Archives; Fig. 42, after *Vanity Fair*, 1915; Fig. 55, after G. M. Hopkins, *Plat Book of the City of Cleveland and Suburbs*, 3 vols. (Philadelphia, 1921), 1: pls. 20-21; Fig. 60, © 1991 by Emily S. Rosen.

CONTENTS

FOREWORD

The complex negotiations involved in creating The Cleveland Museum of Art have been long recognized as a potentially fascinating chapter in the city's coming-of-age as a cosmopolitan center, but no one apparently had the energy to attack the question systematically. The many factions and individuals at the heart of the matter, not to mention the many more lurking on the periphery, spread such a wide net that the research required was daunting.

During the past decade, however, Cleveland's origins have been studied anew, and thanks to such distinguished scholars as Walter C. Leedy, Jr., much more is known about the city's impressive architectural accomplishments at the turn of the century. Thus, the time was ripe for the long-needed sorting out of the Museum's origins and the creation of its first building, which opened to an eager, enthusiastic public in 1916.

Professor Leedy's readiness to attack the facts occurred as the Museum was planning its seventy-fifth anniversary celebration for June 7, 1991; so it seemed an ideal time to pursue the study. And the results are all that one might have expected. The drama of the endless manipulations are portrayed with that rare combination of charm and academic method that has long delighted Professor Leedy's students and friends, and nurtured the admiration of his fellow scholars. The Museum is immensely appreciative of the ordered understanding that has emerged from his extensive research.

The appearance of Hubbell and Benes's stately variant of the Beaux-Arts tradition, which certainly the Museum is, must have been a shocker in its day. A neighborhood park was suddenly graced with a building that could stand proudly on any of the great boulevards of the western world. And the Museum building has stood well the test of time. Perhaps the greatest compliment paid this finely proportioned building is the sensitivity with which the architects Hays and Ruth designed the linkage between it and their 1958 addition which doubled the Museum's size, and which was in turn honored by Breuer and Smith when designing the 1971 addition.

The Art Museum owes a great debt of thanks to the Horace Kelley Art Foundation. The Foundation originally funded three-tenths of the construction cost of the 1916 building, and each year ever since it has contributed handsomely to the operating costs of the Museum. In honor of the seventy-fifth anniversary, the Foundation has made a special grant to underwrite the publication of this book. Once again we all thank the Chairman, Hayward K. Kelley, Jr., and his fellow Trustees.

We believe that the correct telling of the story will promote broader awareness of the visionary concern for the quality of life in Cleveland that originally motivated Horace Kelley to leave the greater part of his estate "for the purpose of purchasing land ... [and erecting] a suitable fireproof building to be used forever as a gallery of art," so all could enjoy the "refining and educating influence of art." His estate joined that of John Huntington to create the Museum building, which remains a source of pride to all who pause on Euclid Avenue to consider it crowning the slopes of the Fine Arts Garden.

Evan H. Turner, *Director*

PREFACE

Since coming to Cleveland, I have been struck that there are so few definitive studies on the history of the city's urban environment and of her significant architectural contributions. The seventy-fifth anniversary of the opening of The Cleveland Museum of Art seemed to be a propitious moment to investigate the rationale that lay behind the design of its superb building and its location in Wade Park.

This study was at first intended to be article length, but I soon realized that the complexity and importance of the subject warranted a full, contextual approach. By presenting a more detailed account I hope to enrich our understanding of why The Cleveland Museum of Art has emerged as a premier institution and a vital educational force in the community. These aspirations were paramount in the minds of the original decision-makers: lawyers, businessmen, museum professionals, and architects. During the planning and design process realities, which were constantly readjusted to ethics and values, determined the Museum's architectural form.

Several people assisted me in ferreting out significant archival material: Virginia Krumholz, Archivist of The Cleveland Museum of Art, and her assistants Ruth Connell and Philip Haas; Maureen Melton, Archivist at the Museum of Fine Arts, Boston; Karen Shafts, Boston Public Library; John Grabowski and Dean Zimmerman of the Western Reserve Historical Society; and my graduate assistant, Paul Miklowski. Stephen Krivanka, an Engineering Foreman at The Cleveland Museum of Art, led me through every nook and cranny of the building.

The College of Graduate Studies of the Cleveland State University granted computer hardware, while the College of Arts and Sciences helped defray the cost of a research trip to Boston. The secretary of the Art Department, Dianne Hlavacek, carefully proofread the initial draft.

I had the good fortune to attend a National Endowment for the Humanities Summer Institute on architectural theory held at the University of Illinois, Urbana-Champaign, where I had continuous thought-provoking discussions with fellow participant Helen Searing of Smith College on the architecture of museums. To all, I am deeply grateful.

W. C. L.

THE BIG DREAM

The Cleveland Museum of Art opened in 1916. The design and construction of this splendid building marked a turning point in museum architecture. Here, for the first time, contemporary objectives for an art museum were not only recognized but, more important, were decisive in the design process. Consequently, a building of utility and beauty was created, and The Cleveland Museum of Art's building codified the principles and procedures that informed the design of American art museums during the next decade.[1]

At that time, Cleveland was the sixth largest city in the United States, one of the very richest in proportion to population, and was a recognized leader in municipal government. Known nationally as a progressive city, Cleveland, however, lagged behind cities like Buffalo and Toledo in establishing an art museum. While there had been a desire to build an art gallery since the 1870s, unique-to-Cleveland historical factors prevented this desire from being more promptly realized.

Founded in 1796, it was only in the 1820s, when Cleveland began to emerge from her log-cabin days, that an interest and even a market for art began to take shape. Not until the last quarter of the nineteenth century, however, when Cleveland had gained industrial might and its population had dramatically increased, did an appreciation of art truly blossom. By this time, great fortunes were accumulating and Cleveland's wealthy, like those of other great American cities, began to enjoy world travel. This experience fueled such an interest in art and especially in art collecting that, like libraries, museums achieved the status of essential components of urban culture and metropolitan life. That this was true not only for Cleveland, but across the nation, is demonstrated by the tripling between 1876 and 1919 of the number of museums in the United States.[2]

Many exhibitions of art were held in temporary locations in Cleveland during the 1870s and early 1880s. One of the most enterprising occurred in 1882 when Sarah M. Kimball, at her spacious Euclid Ave-

Figure 1. Henry Clay Ranney, one of Cleveland's leading lawyers, was an influential champion, as well as decision-maker, in the events leading to the establishment of The Cleveland Museum of Art. He served as a Trustee for all three estates.

nue residence, opened an exhibition of her own art collection, acquired mostly on trips to England. She hoped "to stimulate such an interest in the fine arts as shall ripen into the institution of a museum in Cleveland...." She was helped in this endeavor by several "zealous ladies of the city," and judging from newspaper accounts, the event was an unqualified success. She called her home the temporary gallery of "The Cleveland Museum of Art." By this action, Mrs. Kimball's group hoped to entice a Cleveland philanthropist into donating a fireproof museum building, in which they proposed to place their own collections on permanent exhibition.[3]

Little did Sarah Kimball know that a year earlier, in 1881, Hinman B. Hurlbut had decided to leave a significant amount of money for a museum. It was not until his will was probated in April 1884 that Clevelanders were given their first real hope that a museum would in fact be established. Hurlbut envisioned that the majority of his estate, then estimated at close to $1,200,000—an extraordinary sum for the day—and his highly acclaimed art collection would go toward an art gallery. Nonetheless, since by his will he set up his estate as a trust with the income to provide a life annuity for his wife, the funds earmarked for the museum would not become available until after her death. But this did not mean that plans for the future museum did not proceed, for he named three Trustees: a lawyer, Henry C. Ranney; Judge James D. Cleveland of the city; and William E. Miller of Elyria, Ohio.[4] Of the three, Henry C. Ranney (Figure 1) was the most active in pursuing Hurlbut's dream during the late 1880s, when he spent four summers in Europe visiting galleries to educate himself on the subject of museums.[5]

Hinman Hurlbut's main philanthropic interest up to the time he wrote his will had been in hospital charity and medical education (he also bequeathed $200,000 to Cleveland City Hospital, now Lakeside Hospital, an institution that he had founded, and earlier he had established the Hurlbut professorship of natural sciences at Western Reserve College).[6]

Hurlbut's interest in health care arose partly because of his own poor health. His search for rest and recreation led to an extended European tour from 1865 to 1868, during which time his interest in art and collecting matured. His wife, Jane Elizabeth, was also interested in art and may have stimulated his collecting activities; the newspapers specifically mentioned the great masterpieces Mrs. Hurlbut purchased after her husband's death on her annual trips to England, which were added to the collection.[7] At that time, art collecting was considered to be an appropriate way of achieving status and prestige in the community; it was the visible sign of a cultured person. Furthermore, noblesse oblige was the behavior expected by a society descended from "old New England stock."

In spite of the hope generated by the Hurlbut bequest of 1884, by 1890 Cleveland was only marginally closer to acquiring an art museum, although an understanding of the importance of art for the city continued to grow. A greater number of exhibitions were held, and in the area of art education the Western Reserve School of Design for Women, which was founded by Mrs. Kimball in her home in 1882,[8] was reconstituted into the Cleveland School of Art with a separate Board of Trustees. Then, it became affiliated with Adelbert College of Western Reserve University early in 1888.[9] A competitor school, The Cleveland Art Club, organized in 1876, was incorporated in 1889. Its aim was to offer art instruction up to a level attained by foreign schools, to give lectures, and to hold exhibitions to encourage the public understanding and appreciation of art. As the club had no endowment, expenses were completely covered by the membership and, to keep fees affordable, officers and instructors in evening classes received no pay.[10]

This increasing focus on art no doubt fostered a second large bequest for an art gallery by Horace A. Kelley in 1890. Just over a month before his death, Kelley consulted with Judge James M. Jones, who obtained information and studied the feasibility and propriety of his plans.[11] Only eight days before his death on November 26, 1890—the day before

Thanksgiving Day—Kelley signed a will in which he left the majority of his estate "for the purpose of purchasing land and the erection thereof in the city of Cleveland of a suitable fireproof building to be used forever as a gallery of art for the reception and exhibition of fine paintings, drawings and sculpture, either purchased, donated or loaned, and said building also to be used in part as a school or college for designing, drawing, painting and other fine arts and for the advancement of the same...." He further stipulated that a corporation be formed to achieve those stated objectives and that it be named "The National Gallery of Fine Arts and College of Instruction of Cleveland, Ohio, or any other suitable name that [his] trustees may select."[12]

In slightly over two weeks, therefore, Judge Jones formulated and drafted a complex will and, most significantly for future developments, he convinced Kelley to alter his original idea of giving the bulk of his estate to an existing institution.[13] Which institution he had thus intended to benefit, Jones did not say, but it was well known in the community that Adelbert College was seeking a donation of $100,000 for an art gallery, building, and endowment for the Cleveland School of Art.[14] Not only was Adelbert College under Presbyterian domination at the time, and not, therefore, a neutral body—many realized that the study of art demanded a completely free intellectual environment—but Kelley believed in the "refining and educating influence of art, art instruction and art galleries to which *all the people can have access* [italics mine]...."[15] In order to ensure the achievement of this goal, Judge Jones recommended that a new corporation be formed—one that would stand alone. Not recognizing Kelley's intent, two days after Kelley's will was probated, a Trustee of the Cleveland School of Art and President Charles Franklin Thwing of Western Reserve University suggested that Kelley's bequest be consolidated with the school.[16] A day later several Art School Trustees met "behind closed doors" to discuss severing their ties with Western Reserve University, thus reversing their objective of two weeks earlier (before they knew about Kelley's bequest) to bring the Art School entirely into the University by abandoning their charter and dissolving their Board of Trustees.[17] They thought that if they were an independent art school, they could profit from Kelley's bequest. And they eventually did, although only to a limited extent.

While Kelley's bequest was large, his objectives for both a school and a gallery were even larger. It was immediately recognized that it would be difficult to attain those objectives with the resources available. President Thwing was quick to point out that the $500,000 expected from the Kelley estate would not provide for a great gallery; he reported that even little Raphaels were then selling for $750,000.[18]

Kelley, however, viewed his gallery as a nucleus around which other gifts could cluster, ranging from a single work of art to huge amounts of money. This concept was immediately picked up by the press, which reported that more than one person then living had made a will in which the art gallery project was remembered to the tune of a large sum and implied that all the bequests should be combined.[19] Gifts were conditioned by Kelley's directive to the future corporation: "it is my wish that no work of art unless of acknowledged merit be admitted to said gallery." Today it is normal for museums to have restrictions, but at that time it was not considered good etiquette for museums to look into a gift horse's mouth. His objective of an important institution is also reflected in the name he suggested: "National Gallery of Fine Arts."

The idea of restricting works of art acquired to those of merit may have come to Kelley—or to Jones who studied museums for Kelley—by observing what happened at the Metropolitan Museum of Art in New York. As a result of a permissive acquisitions policy, its building was overcrowded with many pictures having neither value nor interest but occupying valuable space. Furthermore, many donors demanded that their collections, even if composed of disparate items, be exhibited together. And, as many were accepted with such conditions, there was no power to remove

them.[20] A version of Kelley's policy was ultimately reflected in the size of the projected gallery, and it allowed the Trustees to determine how the collection was to be arranged: whether by department (objects of the same culture or time period grouped together) or by groupings of disparate objects, thereby affecting the architectural layout.

Horace Kelley reportedly was a man of "habitual reserve."[21] Perhaps because of this he saw no reason for perpetuating his name or commemorating his family by naming the gallery after himself, although that was, and still is, a traditional condition for gifts. But he had another objective in mind: he hoped to encourage future donations. According to contemporary press reports: "no patron or benefactor will have reason to feel that his gift is hidden by the fame of an earlier or larger bequest."[22] This line of reasoning was continually challenged in succeeding years and was only resolved, after much bickering, when the present organization was incorporated in 1913 as The Cleveland Museum of Art.

Kelley named Judge Jones, Alfred S. Kelley (a cousin), and Henry C. Ranney as Trustees. A solid rather than a brilliant lawyer, Ranney possessed a mental poise that allowed him to reach rational conclusions with force and clarity. He excelled in corporate law.[23] Ranney's appointment may have been guided, however, by more than respect for his legal abilities. Since Ranney was also a Trustee of the Hurlbut estate, Kelley's action may have indicated a hope that the estates might be combined—a suggestion perhaps originating with Jones—providing that the lawyers could work out the legal technicalities. If this were not the case, it seems unduly precipitous that on the day that Kelley's will was probated the *Cleveland Leader* reported that a Trustee of the Hurlbut estate had said that an amalgamation of the Hurlbut and Kelley bequests would be made and that the Trustees of both estates would meet together.

In a move that was unusual for the time, Kelley consulted fully with his wife as plans developed for his bequest, and Judge Jones later reported that he considered the city to be largely indebted to her for this magnificent gift.[24] Mrs. Kelley inherited her husband's personal property, a life annuity of $4,000 per year, and a summer residence in Pasadena, California. She readily consented to his wishes, as she waived her right of notice as the sole next of kin on the day that Kelley's will was probated. The role that women played in events leading to the formation of the Art Museum was, it turns out, substantial.

The expected future impact of Kelley's gift was immediately articulated in the press. These reports provide insight on an art museum's perceived role in the community in the late nineteenth century. According to the *Cleveland Leader*:

The refinements and graces of life cluster and flourish around such a center, and the city will be far more metropolitan, far more independent and enlightened, than ever before. Nothing else in Cleveland will give such distinction to the city which is soon to be the metropolis of Ohio. No other attraction will be so strong to persons of culture and refinement, from without its limits. Within a few years the art museum, so long desired and now assured, will be the chief pride of the community. It will go far toward making art popular and the appreciation of art common, and it will serve to balance somewhat the purely commercial and material development of Cleveland. Such institutions are the noblest of monuments and the finest of memorials. They earn the heartfelt gratitude of every enlightened man and woman, and do only good continually.[25]

Although few had reason to doubt the full success of Kelley's plans, much work had to be done by his Trustees. First, the bequest was entirely in land and buildings, which could either be sold outright, if capital was needed, or rented to produce income. As a result, there were virtually no liquid assets on hand, and the Trustees were responsible for paying Kelley's widow $4,000 per year directly from the rental income received from the property, which was then expected to exceed $16,000 per annum.[26] During her lifetime, therefore, this annuity was in effect a lien against the estate and, as such, "clouded" the title of any land sold. This circumstance made it more diffi-

cult not only to find buyers but to sell the holdings at maximum prices.

Second, Kelley made an unusual provision in his will giving the City of Cleveland the right to purchase a 40-foot wide strip of land to extend Bank Street (now West 6th) south from Superior Street to Michigan Street in the flats for $50,000, which would go to the Museum. (This parcel now lies in the Tower City District.) What motivated him to make this specific bequest is not known; perhaps he expected his other property in the vicinity to increase in value dramatically, thus adding to the funds available for the art gallery to a larger extent than if the improvement were not made.[27] Since 1885 this proposed street extension had been seen as an economic stimulus to businesses in the area. Some questioned the viability of the street because of the steep grade going down into the flats, but almost everyone recognized that Bank Street should be extended, although some citizens felt that the cost should be borne by the owners of the real estate who would profit from the enormous increase in value if the proposed extension were made, rather than by the taxpayers.

Since the strip of land was worth much more than $50,000 on the open market, perhaps as much as $200,000, a lobby developed amongst those who felt the public would be better off if the city refused to accept Kelley's generous offer, so the land could be sold for market value, thereby increasing the funds available for the Museum by an additional $150,000.[28] Cleveland's Superintendent of Public Schools, Lewis W. Day, strongly concurred:

I may be selfish, but I would be in favor of having every dollar ... go to the cause of art. The proposed repository of works of art would be educating, refining, and beneficial in every sense of the word. With our public library, which is doing a grand work, our common schools, colleges, and universities, an art gallery and museum would completely round out the system of education.[29]

Ranney, however, declined to express an opinion on which course of action the city should take. Claiming he had not studied the matter, he only said:

Art is broad. It is confined to no section. When people go to a city, even if they spend only an hour or two there, the first question they ask is, What are the attractions? And principal among all attractions stands an art gallery. It is of great value to a city.[30]

Toward the middle of January 1891, however, the Trustees argued before a special City Council committee set up to investigate the proposed purchase that the city should not buy the parcel.[31] They concluded that a nonacceptance would yield more money to put into the gallery fund.[32] But the committee sided with the local businessmen, and voted to recommend acceptance to City Council, citing as added reasons that the street would give fire protection to the large business interests and that the City Armory would be greatly benefitted.[33]

The public debate heated up. Women in the city questioned why a petition remonstrating against the acceptance was not circulated for their signatures, and the Franklin Club—a forum devoted to discussing government policies—came out against opening the street. As a result of these concerted efforts, Mayor George W. Gardner said he would veto the ordinance if passed. Consequently, City Council postponed taking action,[34] although the total cost of the street's construction was determined.[35] After years of debate, in September 1899 the land was appropriated for the street[36] by City Council and an application to assess compensation was filed in the Court of Insolvency. A twelve-member jury assessed compensation and damages at $100,000.[37] The city, however, was not able to make final payment until October 1904—it had to raise the money. Nonetheless, it agreed to pay interest on this debt, which amounted to an additional $29,850.[38] Although this delayed payment contributed to postponing construction, it substantially increased the other resources available.

In December 1890 there was great hope and anticipation that a gallery would shortly be built. Ranney publicly stated that within a year or two a suitable site would be selected and that a building would be under construction for a national art gallery. No mention

was made of an art school.[39] His remarks were conditioned by the fact that all the real estate in the Kelley legacy could, of course, be sold at once, but that a great deal of it was located in a part of the city that was constantly increasing in value.[40] The Kelley Trustees realized that it was impossible to furnish much of an art gallery for $500,000, let alone to provide an endowment to support it. An effort to maximize resources, therefore, mitigated against selling much of the property at that time. Also, Mrs. Kelley had use of the Kelley homestead on Willson Avenue (now East 55th Street) during her lifetime. The downtown property could not be quickly sold because buyers were difficult to find and, of greater significance, downtown was not then witnessing a "boom." Only the lots located in Newburgh along Tod Street (now East 65th Street in Cleveland) could be sold when the opportunity presented itself. By following this course of action, the Trustees had to pay a few minor bequests, totaling $25,000, and Mrs. Kelley's annuity out of rental income, so it would be at least two years before they would have a positive cash flow.[41]

Meanwhile, by the end of December 1890, the Trustees were besieged with offers of "help." Anxious-to-sell property owners and enterprising real estate agents in the city approached them with proposals for sites. Besides that, they were continually tormented by hosts of applicants for every position: from janitor, to a woman who applied for the superintendency of the oil painting department, to men who offered to take charge of the entire operation. In reaction, the Trustees decided to do nothing until they had a clear idea of what they should do, although Ranney, it was reported, had "very definite mind pictures of what the gallery shall be," notions he had developed while traveling in Europe, visiting the British Isles, Germany, Switzerland, and France, on behalf of the Hurlbut estate.[42] Hermon A. Kelley, a cousin of the late Horace, however, who had been recently appointed secretary to the Kelley Trustees, spoke without authority—but no doubt to test the waters—when he remarked,

I am certain that the proposed art gallery will not be built down town. The smoke and dust of the city would injure ... art works ... marble statuary would become begrimed with smoke ... it would be necessary to clean the oil paintings every three or four years, which would eventually ruin them. It is probable that the gallery will be located some place in the East End.[43]

The question of location generated debate and concern, for many people wanted the gallery to be downtown. To counter their opponents the Trustees requested that Chicago art critic Edward R. Garczynski—after visiting Cleveland and meeting with the Trustees—write a letter, which they later released for publication, pointing out that it was not dirt but smoke that ruins paintings. (A chemical change produced by the sulphur in coal when burned unites with the oxygen and water in the air and forms sulfuric acid—"acid rain.")[44] Nonetheless, conservation of the collection was a major concern. In the planning process, scientific arguments were put forth and eminent authorities consulted. Besides environmental concerns, the Trustees were looking for a site that would be adaptable for future, as well as present, needs and one that was as accessible as possible to the public.[45] Knowing that they did not have sufficient assets for the task at hand, the Trustees openly advertised their hope that a generous individual—following Kelley's example—would donate a site for the gallery.[46]

In turn, the Trustees were rigorously lobbied for support by both the Art Club and the Cleveland School of Art, whose rivalry was open and vociferous. In February 1891 the Trustees accepted an invitation to visit the Art Club, then housed in city hall, where they observed two drawing classes: one on still life, the other working from a draped model.[47] Club members admitted that it was pretty poor pickings for an artist who attempted to get along without having a fixed revenue as a teacher.[48] The Trustees also held informal talks with the Art School about the matter of a union. But as yet the relationship of the school to the university was still an open question and, furthermore, the school was at that time coping with an internal scandal.[49] The issue was settled in June 1891, when the school's Trustees voted to secede from the university, thus putting themselves in a position to unite with the Kelley interests.[50] In the end, however, the Kelley Trustees decided to support the School of Art instead of the Art Club. Since Mrs. Kelley had resolved to live in California, they could allow the school to use the Kelley house on Willson Avenue rent free—from the summer of 1892.[51] This decision, although partly based on favoritism—Ranney was a past president of the Western Reserve School of Design for Women, the predecessor of the Cleveland School of Art—was probably also based on the difference in character between the organizations. The school had the reputation of being elitist[52] which gave it an aura of refinement.

A few years earlier, Mary D. Warner of Painesville, Ohio, had bequeathed to the City of Cleveland $5,000 and some oil paintings for an art gallery. Since the city had no right to construct one, it was tacitly agreed by the elected city officials and the Trustees of the Hurlbut estate that the two bequests should be combined. It was understood that the Kelley estate would be united with the Hurlbut estate when it became available and until that time that the Kelley estate would form the nucleus around which gifts could be added. Based on this understanding, the city pursued and won a case in the Ohio Supreme Court giving it the right to accept the bequest from Mrs. Warner's estate and to "pass it through" at the right time to the art gallery project. Although the city wanted a greater role in the project, the Trustees proceeded independently.[53]

Meanwhile, the Kelley Trustees were beginning to think about what kind of building they wanted. After seeing the Metropolitan Museum of Art in New York, they decided it not only had an ugly appearance but was not at all adapted to its purpose, since the whole was poorly lighted. Apparently, they did not like the building's style, which was Ruskinian Gothic; their opinion was formed before the World's Fair of 1892-1893 made academic classicism the popular

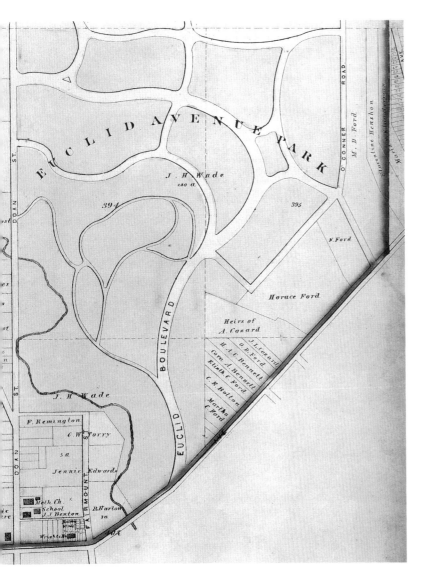

Figure 2. Occupying a deep ravine, Wade Park was developed by Jeptha H. Wade beginning in 1872. It was a private park open to the public.

style for public buildings. In the early 1890s, therefore, the Trustees reached two conclusions. First, the gallery must have architectural beauty; and second, to obtain the best light, the building should not be over two stories in height. They based this second conclusion on the fact that the best light attainable for the purpose of viewing art comes from skylights. (Top lighting was generally preferred for painting galleries, because it corresponds to the prevailing direction of light under which artists worked.) In 1891 Brooklyn was contemplating building an art gallery and museum, and the Kelley Trustees watched with interest to see what they, who had the opportunity to study the bad features of the Metropolitan, would do to create a model gallery.[54] In late April, during a stay in Washington, Ranney called on "Professor" Henry W. Elliott. This Cleveland artist and naturalist, who fought to save the fur-seal herds on the Pribilof Islands, was associated with the Smithsonian Institute. Elliott advised Ranney that a museum aside from "mere exhibition" must be educational, thus reinforcing ideas earlier expressed by Cleveland's artists. The founders of the Smithsonian proceeded slowly, lived within their incomes, and only finished portions of the building as they were needed. This was the behavioral model that the Cleveland Trustees adopted.[55] Being good businessmen and lawyers, they had no other choice.

Also, around this time the Trustees brought Halsey C. Ives of the St. Louis Art Museum and School of Fine Arts to Cleveland for consultation about the building.[56] A figure of national importance, Ives had established an art education program in St. Louis and later served as Chief of the Department of Fine Arts at the Chicago World's Fair in 1892-93.[57]

By late 1891 the Trustees had decided on a site, and they wrote to J. H. Wade, who was then in Europe, to ask if they could purchase a tract of land within Wade Park, to which he and his wife had title.[58] Wade had received this land from his grandfather, Jeptha H. Wade (d. 1890), who had excluded it from his gift to the city. When the latter had offered

to donate Wade Park (Figure 2) to the city in 1881—
the deed was not transferred until 1882—he had excluded up to eight acres of unspecified park land,
upon which he had intended to establish a college. It
was only after a landscape artist had made plans for
changes and improvements in the park consistent
with the land's natural formation that Wade had chosen the exact site he desired (Figure 3).[59]

Since 1880 Jeptha Wade had been in contact with
the non-sectarian liberal Theological School in
Meadville, Pennsylvania, which he intended to bring
to Cleveland. In one letter (November 6, 1880) to
Henry W. Bellows—a clergyman of national stature
who was a proponent of this endeavor—Wade described his vision:

Mr. Case left property worth about $1,000,000 to estab
lish the "Case School of Applied Science." ... It is expected
and almost certain that the Presbyterians will remove the
"Western Reserve College" from Hudson to this city. Now
if the Institute from Meadville should also come here and
be made equal to the others, would not all reap advantages
by being together and would it not make Cleveland such
an educational center as to attract endowments and sup
port that they could hardly expect if separate and in coun
try villages?[60]

Sixteen days later he wrote again to Bellows: "it will
be a monument to live after I am dead.... I may want
to spend more on the building than to some others
might seem provident.... I want to be sure of its success." Wade proposed not only to endow the college
handsomely and erect a suitably symbolic building—
"it might not be policy or economy for us to admit
any inferiority"—but to establish one or two professorships in "Spiritual Philosophy" that would be devoted to an investigation of "what is claimed to be
communication between departed spirits and those
yet in the body." His aim was to uncover such communication as either a gigantic fraud or a demonstration of the immortality of man. Wade had a personal
objective for this: his son Randall had died in 1876,
and he sought to communicate with him through
"automatic writing."[61]

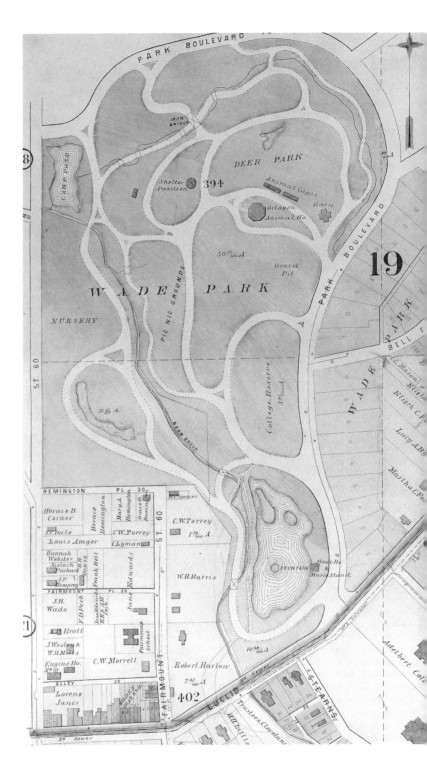

Figure 3. Wade Park was donated to the City of Cleveland in 1882 by Jeptha H. Wade on the condition that the paths and drives be reorganized following the natural contours of the land. He reserved ownership of the parcel marked "college reserve."

Figure 4. Wade Park, looking south across the artificial lake to Adelbert College, about 1890. Wade chose the site for his intended college so that it would be visually connected with the other educational institutions in the area and with the city as a whole.

The site Jeptha H. Wade chose within Wade Park visually reinforced his objective for the college to be part of a larger educational center. It was a kidney-shaped site (a little over 4 acres), about 700 feet long and 350 feet wide, located 650 feet north of Euclid Avenue (Figure 3). Its short side was just north of the artificial lake in Wade Park; the entire site was surrounded by boulevards. It had good visibility from the corner of Euclid Avenue and Fairmount Street (now East 107th). Furthermore, it was on an elevation facing Adelbert College and Case School of Applied Science, and it could be seen from the College for Women (Figure 4). By 1884 the negotiations with Meadville had gone up in smoke—Wade wanted the right to name the college but the Trustees objected—and, as a result, the idea to found a college fell into limbo.

It is easy to suppose how Clevelanders would have reacted to the location of a theological institute in the middle of a public park. The newspapers of the time even discussed the imprudence of associating in any way a scientific school like Case with a Presbyterian college like the Western Reserve. While this site had no intended use when J. H. Wade received it, decorum demanded it should not be sold or given for just any purpose. Both Western Reserve University and the School of Art wanted it, and the Park Commission tried to procure it as a site for the Soldiers' and Sailors' monument.[62] One of the Kelley Trustees, James M. Jones, had been attorney for the Western Union Telegraph Company when Jeptha Wade was president of the company and, privately, had defended Randall Wade—J. H. Wade's father—in a slander trial. (He was accused of calling Rosa Benton a strumpet. She was employed by The Crittenden Company—a competitor of a jewelry store in which Randall owned an interest.)[63] This personal relationship between the Wade family and one of the Kelley Trustees certainly gave them entrée.[64]

When the Kelley Trustees first approached J. H. Wade, he indicated that the purchase price for the parcel would be no less than $100,000, but if they wanted the parcel, money would be no obstacle. After Wade decided to donate the land, he had the deed, which he signed on December 23, 1892, delivered to Ranney's office on the afternoon of December 24. Just in time, of course, so that the gift could be announced in the newspapers on Christmas Day.[65] The deed states that he gave the land for the purpose of "aiding in securing the benefit of united action in the use of all property and funds that are now or may be available for the promotion and advancement of art and for the construction and maintenance of an art gallery and school in my native city of Cleveland...."

Besides these reasons, other factors influenced Wade's decision to donate the land. First, he had acquired a taste for art,[66] which may have come to him naturally since his grandfather started off as a portrait painter. This curiosity had been nurtured when he went on a grand tour of Europe at age thirteen with his father, Randall, who was forced to travel abroad to minimize the publicity surrounding the slander trial.[67] Second, J. H. Wade was developing Cleveland's most exclusive residential district, the adjoining Wade Park Allotment, and a nearby art gallery would have been viewed as an amenity by the upper classes. Third, a strong lobby was developing in the city to discharge, by appropriation if necessary, Wade's right to the park site, so that the whole could be used for park land.[68] Fourth, the Trustees of William Gordon's estate expressed a willingness to give his art collection to the Wade Park gallery and $5,000 to the building fund. So a confluence of factors, rather than any single one, most likely led Wade to make this magnificent gift to the people of Cleveland. An editorial in the *Cleveland Leader* illustrates a contemporary view on the appropriateness of the site to its function:

a magnificent temple of art will stand in a beautiful park which is already the most popular outdoor resort in Cleveland.... Colleges will be in immediate proximity.... The visitor can turn from the glories of art to the loveliness of nature.... All the surroundings ... most befit the study and enjoyment of the beautiful ... a feast of the beautiful is bet-

ter enjoyed when it is a little apart from the associations and surroundings of business life.[69]

In contrast to a downtown city block this location, besides being clean and free from noise, offered greater possibilities for expansion, could provide ample natural light, and even better, lessened the threat to the works of art from any fire spreading from adjoining structures, which was a major problem in the nineteenth century. All these reasons had been similarly recognized during the 1870s in the planning of the Metropolitan Museum of Art, which was placed in Central Park.

The choice of the Wade Park site, however, did not go unchallenged, and opposition continued until actual construction began. Opponents argued that while visitors to the city would surely find it, Clevelanders would look at it from afar and visit it only once a month. They demanded a downtown location where people could often stop in and stay long—not one on the outskirts of the city. The journey out to Wade Park and back from downtown took an hour. The experience of museums in other cities supported their argument that convenience, not quality, was the single most critical factor influencing attendance.[70]

When the site was acquired in late 1892, it was still too early to make any precise building plans. The Trustees indicated, however, that it would only be built in part at first, according to current requirements, and that additions would be made in the future without detracting from the symmetry of the whole.[71] They already knew what they wanted: a monumental symmetrical building. The Trustees were strong-willed men; any architect they hired would have to give physical form to their vision.

Seven years passed before the Kelley Trustees set up a corporation for building a museum. Meanwhile, a third bequest—the largest—was made for founding an art museum. Although it had been rumored in the papers in 1890 that a benefactor would leave a large sum of money for a such a purpose, it was not until John Huntington died in 1893 that his intentions became public knowledge. Since Henry C. Ranney was named as one of the executors of his estate,[72] and he was a long-standing confidant and legal advisor to John Huntington, Ranney knew of Huntington's intentions well before his will was probated.

In his will, written in 1889, Huntington created the "John Huntington Art and Polytechnic Trust" to provide a "gallery and museum" and a "free evening polytechnic school." Immediately after Huntington's death, Henry Ranney began to work aggressively and openly to unite all three estates in the belief that Cleveland should have one "magnificent" museum instead of two or three smaller ones. The motivation behind his goal was the belief that buildings endure, revealing to every passerby the standards of taste and customs of the period of their origin, and that they not only give a city its actual and remembered outline, but that they record the stages of its development and its quality.

Under the terms of Huntington's will, the art trust was to receive 19 percent of the net earnings of the estate each year, out of which the art trust was obligated to make a one-time payment of $70,000 to the John Huntington Benevolent Trust, a fund he had created on his fifty-seventh birthday for the benefit of Cleveland's charitable institutions. After the death of his widow and his last child, the estate was to be equally divided between his grandchildren then living and the art trust. Although Huntington's will was probated in 1893, no distributions were made for several years, until Hannah Beck Huntington (one of Huntington's children) and other interested parties instituted court proceedings to force the executors to close their accounts. Only under court order did they begin to pay out income in 1896-1897. (According to court records, the delay was caused by Huntington's apparently large personal indebtedness. Several of the claims filed against his estate were legally disputed by the executors in court.) Final distribution of the assets of Huntington's estate did not occur until 1928.[73]

Not only were Huntington's heirs concerned that the estate was not being settled in a timely manner, but the Board of Directors of the Cleveland Chamber of Commerce appointed an Art Museum Committee in December 1896 to investigate conditions governing the bequests and endeavor to gain their united action. To this end the Trustees of the three Trusts reported to the committee in January 1897. Much to everyone's surprise, their reports indicated that none of them singly or together had sufficient resources in hand to commence construction.[74]

Legal action against the Trustees of Huntington's estate, coupled with the official query from the Cleveland Chamber of Commerce, had only ceremonial effect. Shortly thereafter, in March 1897, the Huntington Trust held its first meeting, elected its chairman—Edwin R. Perkins—and received its first funds, $39,401.66,[75] which were hardly enough for any undertaking. Their next official meeting, held a year later in April 1898, was more consequential: one of the Trustees, Judge Samuel E. Williamson, introduced a motion resolving that the Huntington Trustees "will co-operate with the trustees of the estate of Horace A. Kelley or any corporation which they may cause to be formed, in the formation of one institution as far as the provisions of the will ... will legally permit." This qualification was specifically included in the resolution because they did not know if it would be possible to get around a provision in Huntington's will specifying that the nine Huntington Trustees "shall have the entire management and control of said gallery."[76]

With assurance from the Huntington Trust that united action was now possible and not just desirable, the Kelley Trustees proceeded to execute their duty as Trustees of Kelley's will: they formed a not-for-profit corporation in February 1899, "to erect, establish and maintain ... a [art] gallery ... and also a museum of natural or other curiosities of art; the establishment and maintenance of a Polytechnic School and an academic School of Art, and for all or any of these purposes to receive gifts ... and apply such in accordance with the expressed wishes ... of the donors." Of the five incorporators, two were Trustees of the Huntington Trust.[77] Judge Williamson had the idea to have, as far as possible, the same members on the Boards of the various trusts. Two years later—when supposed legal technicalities prevented united action—he reflected: "I had supposed that the reliance for harmonious administration of the art collection and schools provided for in the various trusts are to be affected largely and mainly by having the same persons interested in the success of all of them as far as possible."[78]

The corporation set up by the Kelley Trustees was known as the Cleveland Museum of Art from its inception in 1899 until 1913, when they agreed to change its name to the Horace Kelley Art Foundation. To avoid confusion with the present corporation, however, it is henceforth referred to as the Kelley Foundation.

At their first meeting, on May 15, 1899, the incorporators approved the regulations presented by Ranney, which specified that membership would be limited to twenty and that an eighteen-member Board of Trustees would be elected. Furthermore, they nominated a roll of thirteen members, naturally enough selecting from Cleveland's most distinguished citizens—those who were in a position to help with the enterprise—including J. H. Wade, who gave the site; John D. Rockefeller; George H. Worthington; the noted lawyers Samuel Williamson and William B. Sanders; Samuel Mather; Charles F. Brush, the inventor of the arc lamp; and Liberty Holden, owner and publisher of the *Cleveland Plain Dealer*. Eventually, Brush, Rockefeller, and one other declined to serve, citing frequent absence from the city and pressing business engagements that prevented them from giving proper attention to the duties of Trustees.

The Trustees of the Kelley Foundation met on May 31, 1899; Ranney was elected President, Jones and Wade Vice-Presidents. They elected an executive committee, which included Edwin Perkins, Chairman of the Huntington Trust. The Foundation had no more official meetings that year, but on January 13, 1900, they held a meeting at which three new members were elected to fill vacancies: Henry R. Hatch,

J. G. W. Cowles, and Charles F. Olney. Both Hatch and Cowles were deeply involved in the city's commercial development and were no doubt elected to lend their expertise in selling the land in the Kelley estate, which was about to be transferred to the new corporation.[79] On the other hand, Olney was a local expert in art who had a custom-designed gallery built to house his own collection.

On January 31, 1900, the Kelley Foundation appointed a building committee of six "to investigate the method of employing architects and procuring plans and its recommendations as to the best method of procedure in going about the work of building a museum of art."[80] They also received from the Trustees of the Kelley estate the deed for the Wade Park site for the Museum and deeds for five parcels of land, still unsold; $36,910.31 in cash; bills receivable amounting to $1,950; and the rights to award in court of insolvency in the proceeding instituted by the City of Cleveland for the appropriation of Bank Street.[81] One of the deeds was for Kelley's house on Willson Avenue, which the Kelley Trustees had allowed the Cleveland School of Art to occupy rent free. The new Kelley Foundation agreed to continue this arrangement until the property was sold. While the corporation had land, it had very little cash, so a Real Estate Committee[82] was formed to sell the land for the highest prices possible. Over the next few years offers for various parcels were made but often rejected as being too low. Eventually, two parcels were sold to the Van Sweringen interests for the Terminal Tower site in the early 1920s. Around 1900, however, neither the Kelley Foundation nor the Huntington Trust was as yet in a financial position to build.

At the first meeting of the Building Committee on February 3, 1900,[83] Henry W. Elliott proposed that he be hired to investigate art galleries in the United States. After discussion, the committee decided not to employ Elliott, but recognizing a survey as a rational first step, they decided to do it themselves. They proceeded to assemble printed catalogues, prospectuses, and reports from major art galleries, as well as architectural plans and data. By deciding on this two-pronged strategy, they sought to comprehend the intricacies of museum design as related to function. The committee viewed this study as its preparation for choosing an architect and a building style or type.[84] The record book does not note any subsequent official meetings of this committee. More pressing fiscal and legal issues had to be settled first.

In May 1901 Liberty Holden, speaking before the Cleveland Chamber of Commerce in a poetic and visionary tone, related his "dream" for mid-twentieth-century Cleveland: "Magnificent indeed will be the double expression of the group plan when an art museum and the college buildings in the east end shall have been built in such number and with such accommodations as to meet all the wants of higher education ... all cooperating under the university idea and grouped in wisdom for convenience in attendance of laboratory and lecture."[85] (The Group Plan was a scheme to place all the government buildings according to a unified plan, so that the total composition would have greater visual and symbolic importance than any single part. The result can be seen today, in the Mall downtown.)[86] Holden envisioned the essence of urban life being given visual symbolization: business and government on the one hand, education and culture on the other.

In 1897 the Western Reserve Historical Society had moved from Public Square to Euclid Avenue opposite Wade Park. Part of the rationale for the move had been the perceived benefits to be derived from the nearby educational institutions.[87] Planning for the move and the selection of the new site occurred after Henry C. Ranney was elected President of the Society in May 1895.[88] No doubt he was a force in persuading the Society to relocate near the proposed art museum site.

Although good intentions abounded, no actual legal arrangements had been worked out by 1901 to unite the Kelley Foundation, Huntington Trust, and the Hurlbut estate for building one museum. To this end, further legal opinions were sought. Over the years from 1901 to 1905 the Boards of the Huntington Trust and the Kelley Foundation intentionally gained more members in common, thus encouraging a solution. Only one person, however, served on all three boards during this period: Henry Ranney. As such, he was the only link to the Hurlbut estate.

The legal hurdles were defined as: (1) since the Huntington Trust was a personal trust, any property must remain in the control of the Trustees; its Trustees could, however, employ a corporation to run a museum; (2) the Huntington Trust could not make any permanent contract, although it could rent in perpetuity a building constructed for its own use and/or the land beneath it; and (3) the Kelley Foundation had no right, based on its articles of incorporation, to give the Huntington Trust a perpetual lease on its land, although the deed from Wade for the site would presumably allow it. Since the phrase *expressed wish of donors* was contained in the articles, however, this could give power for such a lease and suggested to the lawyers that the articles could be amended to embrace the purpose of leasing or selling for reasons akin to the general objectives of the organization.[89] It was later recalled that the idea for a lease had first been suggested years earlier by Judge Williamson.[90]

Believing that a solution to all the legal obstacles had been found and having $387,462.17 in the bank, the Huntington Trustees officially proposed to the Kelley Foundation in mid-1904: (1) that the Huntington Trustees procure plans for constructing on the Wade Park site a building designed with three sections, each separately owned by the three estates, and (2) that the Huntington Trust would lease in perpetuity the land upon which it would erect its part of the building—its cost not to exceed $500,000—to form part of the completed single art museum as contemplated by Wade's deed of land. When the plans were completed, they would be presented to the Kelley Foundation for its approval.[91] The idea of building three museums, each under different ownership, that would look like one harmonious whole when finished goes back to at least 1901, when it was suggested as a possible solution by Hermon Kelley.[92] This general concept has a long history in urban buildings. The Huntington Trust intended to build its section first; the other two sections would follow as needed and when funds became available.

To effect this scheme, the Kelley Foundation amended its bylaws and unanimously adopted the Huntington Trust's proposal on June 5, 1905.[93] So assured was everyone that everything would go smoothly from now on, that an announcement was made to the press. Soon, it seemed, even those who could afford it would not have "to go away for that elusive thing called culture."[94]

1. See, for example, John Cotton Dana, *The New Museum* (Woodstock, VT: The Elm Tree Press, 1917), 51, who described the museum as a "building which embodies the best and latest in planning and arrangement ..."; Henry W. Kent, "Museums of Art," *Architectural Forum* 47 (December 1927): 584; and Laurence Vail Coleman, *Museum Buildings* (Washington: American Association of Museums, 1950), 1: 3, affirmed that Cleveland's building ushered in a new period.

2. This figure is an estimate; see George Ellis Burcaw, *Introduction to Museum Work* (Nashville: American Association for State and Local History, 1975), 26.

3. *Cleveland Herald*, July 13, 1882. An advertisement for the exhibition appeared in the *Cleveland Herald* on July 20, 1882. Admission was $.50 on Tuesdays and $.25 on Saturdays. It was also open on Thursdays, but only to patrons and nonresident visitors.

4. Will dated April 27, 1881. Cuyahoga County, Record of Wills, M: 267, April 21, 1884; copy in Will, Hinman Hurlbut file, Corporate, Archives, The Cleveland Museum of Art, (hereafter cited as CMA Archives).

5. *Cleveland Plain Dealer*, December 18, 1890.

6. Biography of Hinman Hurlbut, typescript, undated, unsigned, 21-35, CMA Archives.

7. *Cleveland Leader*, December 12, 1890.

8. The idea was developed that together with her museum a school should be started. See *Cleveland Herald*, August 1, 1882. For a time classes were held in Mrs. Kimball's home studio, then they were moved to City Hall. The School had many women backers. See Mrs. W. A. Ingham, *Women of Cleveland and Their Work* (Cleveland: W. A. Ingham, 1893), 305-306. Formal incorporation came slightly after the first classes were held on November 13, 1882. Henry C. Ranney served as the first president from January 1883 to 1885. See Nancy Coe Wixom, *Cleveland Institute of Art, The First Hundred Years* (Cleveland, 1983), 13.

9. Wixom, *Cleveland Institute of Art*, 15.

10. *Cleveland Plain Dealer*, December 17, 1890. Original course announcements, Cleveland Art Club for 1890-1891 and 1891-1892, vertical file, Ingalls Library of The Cleveland Museum of Art (hereafter cited as CMA Ingalls Library).

11. *Cleveland Leader*, December 12, 1890. Interview with Judge Jones.

12. Kelley's will, probated on December 11, 1890, was witnessed by N. C. McFarland and M. A. Foran. Docket 25, no. 4836, Probate Court; Record of Wills, 16: 323, Cuyahoga County.

13. *Cleveland Leader*, December 12, 1890.

14. *Cleveland Plain Dealer*, December 11, 1890.

15. Quote from Kelley's Will. Will, Horace Kelley file, Corporate, CMA Archives.

16. *Cleveland Plain Dealer*, December 13, 1890.

17. Ibid., December 14, 1890.

18. Ibid., December 13, 1890.

19. *Cleveland Leader*, December 12, 1890.

20. These points were discussed in the Cleveland newspapers; see, for example, *Cleveland Plain Dealer*, March 26, 1891.

21. *Cleveland Plain Dealer*, December 11, 1890.

22. Editorial, *Cleveland Leader*, December 12, 1890.

23. *The Biographical Cyclopaedia and Portrait Gallery with an Historical Sketch of the State of Ohio* (Cincinnati: Western Biographical Publishing Co., 1883-1894), 4: 898-900.

24. *Cleveland Leader*, December 12, 1890.

25. Editorial, ibid., December 12, 1890.

26. Ibid., December 14, 1890, citing affidavit filed with the court.

27. Ibid.

28. Ibid., December 13 and 21, 1890.

29. Ibid., December 14, 1890.

30. *Cleveland Plain Dealer*, December 15, 1890.

31. Ibid., January 11, 1891; see Cleveland, *City Council Proceedings*, Communication to Council from Mayor George Gardner, December 15, 1890, who suggested the committee be established; J. M. Jones wrote to Mayor Gardner telling him of the details of Kelley's will. The committee was formed on December 15, 1890.

32. *Cleveland Plain Dealer*, January 15, 1891.

33. "Report of the Special Committee on Opening of Bank Street, January 26, 1891." The committee members were H. B. Hannum, C. A. Davidson, and J. A. Robinson. City Council Archives, City of Cleveland.

34. Cleveland, *City Council Proceedings*, January 26, 1891; *Cleveland Plain Dealer*, January 28, 1891.

35. Estimates were made to determine the city's actual cost. See Cleveland, *City Council Proceedings*, February 2, 9, March 2, 1891.

36. September 18, 1899. Cleveland, *List of Streets Accepted by Ordinances, Deed, etc., to June 1, 1900* (Cleveland, 1900), 6-7, copy in the Western Reserve Historical Society. The street only went from Superior to Champlain.

37. Court of Insolvency, no. 356, 1: 364, microfilm record, Cuyahoga County Court House.

38. Court of Insolvency, no. 356, 1: 364, microfilm record, Cuyahoga County Court House; the City Solicitor, Newton D. Baker, calculated the interest on the judgment and worked out the arrangements for payment. See Baker to H. A. Kelley, June 4, 7, and October 1, 1904, Newton D. Baker Papers, MS. 3867, cont. 9, nos. 189, 218, 738, Western Reserve Historical Society.

39. An art school per se was never developed in conjunction with the Museum. Perhaps the Trustees did not feel they had sufficient resources or later that the close proximity of the School of Art would satisfy Kelley's educational goals. However, it is interesting to speculate to what extent the Trustees, who were aligned with the central forces of society—civic boosters and the wealthy who were philanthropically inclined—were opposed to having artists, who were generally antagonistic towards marble palaces where the elite venerated art, in the same building. On this interesting dimension in the development of the museum in America, see Sidney Dillon Ripley, *The Sacred Grove: Essays on Museums* (New York: Simon and Schuster, 1969), 72-74.

40. *Cleveland Plain Dealer*, December 15, 1890.

41. Ibid., February 9, 1891.

42. Ibid., December 18, 1890; and *National Cyclopaedia of American Biography* (1893), 3: 217.

43. *Cleveland Leader*, December 28, 1890.

44. He also inspected local art collections—some of which he roundly condemned, others he praised, and he found much to admire in the Hurlbut Collection. *Cleveland Plain Dealer*, April 14, 1891. Garczynski's name was misspelled in the paper. His major publication, it seems, was a book on Sullivan's auditorium building (*Auditorium* [New York, 1890]) which he interpreted in Ruskinian terms. I owe this information to Professor Lauren Weingarten of Florida State University.

45. *Cleveland Leader*, February 16, 1891.

46. *Cleveland Plain Dealer*, February 9, 1891.

47. Ibid., February 17, 1891.

48. Ibid., March 15, 1891.

49. Ibid., March 18, 1891.

50. Ibid., June 4, 1891; Wixom, *Cleveland Institute of Art*, 16.

51. Wixom, *Cleveland Institute of Art*, 16. It was reported that the high ceilings of the magnificent rooms in the Kelley house elevated the students' ideas, and the patina of the black walnut doors, stairways, and furniture made their hands and eyes forever dissatisfied with shoddy and makeshift craftsmanship. See *Cleveland Plain Dealer*, December 20, 1928.

52. Wixom, *Cleveland Institute of Art*, 18.

53. *Cleveland Plain Dealer*, March 26, 1891. The funds were placed into the Mary Warner Art Gallery Trust and by 1915 had grown to over $11,000. See Cleveland, *City Council Proceedings*, file 35372, January 4, 1915. There were continual requests for assistance from this Trust; for example, the Cleveland School of Art sought funds in 1907. Newton D. Baker to Johnson, November 25, 1907: "art gallery funds, being administered by private trustees, have proceeded independently of the City in their projected ... museum." Tom L. Johnson Papers, MS. 3651, Western Reserve Historical Society.

54. *Cleveland Plain Dealer*, March 26, 1891.

55. Ibid., April 26, 1891; for information on Elliott, see *Henry Wood Elliott, 1846-1930: A Retrospective Exhibition* (Anchorage: Anchorage Historical and Fine Arts Museum, 1982), and Kay F. Booth, "Henry W. Elliott," typescript, 1963, William E. Scheele Papers, Archives, Cleveland Museum of Natural History. For a time Elliott was in charge of an exposition for Cleveland's Centennial for which he provided a design for a building to cover three and one-third acres and to cost $180,000. It was intended to include 378 specific exhibits of home manufactures and historical, marine, educational, and women's displays. He worked with a citizens committee which included Liberty Holden and H. R. Hatch, who were later associated with the development of the Art Museum. See Edward A. Roberts, *Official Report of the Centennial Celebration of the Founding of the City of Cleveland and the Settlement of the Western Reserve* (Cleveland: The Cleveland Printing and Publishing Company, 1896), 3.

56. *Museum News* (Toledo) 3, 1 (November 1909).

57. *Dictionary of American Biography*.

58. *Cleveland Leader*, December 25, 1892.

59. Cleveland, *City Council Proceedings*, June 20, 1881. For the letter from Jeptha H. Wade along with a plan of Wade Park as it then existed, see *Cleveland Plain Dealer*, June 21, 1881. The replanning of the park was carried out under the Park Commissioners and was personally approved by Wade. The deed transferred to the city on September 15, 1882. Records of Deeds, 341: 165; and for the plat, see Map Records, 12: 48, Cuyahoga County.

60. Unsigned draft, Wade Family Papers, MS. 3292, cont. 4, Western Reserve Historical Society; for the letter as sent with almost the same wording, see Wade to Henry W. Bellows, November 6, 1880, Henry W. Bellows Papers, Massachusetts Historical Society. Other letters to Bellows from Wade, dated March 10 and July 11, 1881, indicate that the moving of the other schools was not so firmly established and "all hang from day to day."

61. Wade to Bellows, November 22, 1880; December 3, 1880; November 13, 1880, Wade Family Papers, MS. 3292, cont. 4, Western Reserve Historical Society.

62. *Cleveland Plain Dealer*, December 25, 1892.

63. For details, see James M. Wood, "The Wades' Grand Tour," *Cleveland Magazine* 14, 6 (June 1985): 98-108.

64. Further evidence for a close relationship is that both Jones and Ranney were guests at J. H. Wade's wedding in 1878. See "Wedding Party List," Wade Family Papers, MS. 3292, cont. 12, folder 5, Western Reserve Historical Society.

65. *Cleveland Plain Dealer*, December 25, 1892; for title transfer, see Cuyahoga County Records of Deeds, 542: 104-106.

66. When J. H. Wade traveled he often visited art museums. These are documented in little notebooks he kept; for example, in 1876 he visited the Metropolitan Museum of Art and the Academy of Design. See "Cash Account Book 7/5/76-9/16/76," Wade Family Papers, MS. 3292, cont. 12, folder 5, Western Reserve Historical Society.

67. Wood, "The Wades' Grand Tour," 100.

68. See, for example, Editorial, *Cleveland Leader*, March 31, 1891.

69. Ibid., December 25, 1892.

70. See, for example, "Build the Museum Down Town," *The Ohio Architect and Builder* 1, 6 (June 1903): 4. The author specifically argued for including the museum in The Group Plan. He analyzed locational impact on museum attendance at Chicago's Field Museum in comparison to the Art Institute of Chicago, claiming that for each person who visits the former, ten visit the latter. "A Great Museum of Art," ibid., 5, 6 (June 1905): 33. The author pleads for a location closer to the center of the city.

71. *Cleveland Plain Dealer*, December 25, 1892.

72. The others were Edwin R. Perkins, Mariett Huntington, Charles Bingham, and John V. Painter.

73. Docket 32, no. 8182, Probate Court, Cuyahoga County; Common Pleas Court of Cuyahoga County cause 54,725, January 1896, Journal 123, p. 195; Final Report and Settlement of the Executors, March 25, 1902, submitted to Court of Common Pleas; Application for Distribution in Kind, Docket 32, 8182, November 1, 1928; Will, John Huntington file, Harold T. Clark Papers, CMA Archives.

74. The members of the committee were W. R. Warner, chrmn., Stevenson Burke, Charles Brush, L. E. Holden, and J. H. Wade. It was formed following a motion of H. R. Hatch. Minutes of the Board of Directors of the Cleveland Chamber of Commerce, December 10, 1896; Minutes of the Art Museum Committee, January 5, 15, 1897, MS. 3471, cont. 3, Western Reserve Historical Society.

75. An audit of the art trust in 1915 showed that between March 1, 1896, and April 30, 1915, their total receipts (income plus interest) were $1,530,883.19. Total disbursements up to that date were $782,175.71, out of which $560,000 was placed in the fund for construction, $75,000 for the purchase of art works, $32,200 for operating expenses, plus architects' and other fees, see Ernst & Ernst, "Audit Report, John Huntington Art and Polytechnic Trust, April 30, 1915," Business Office, Audits, CMA Archives.

76. Minutes of the John Huntington Art and Polytechnic Trust, March 3, 1897, and April 8, 1898, CMA Archives.

77. James M. Jones, Henry C. Ranney, Edwin R. Perkins, William E. Miller, and Hermon A. Kelley. The articles of incorporation are dated February 27, 1899, and recorded in vol. 73, p. 662, of the Records of Incorporation; see Cleveland Museum of Art [now the Horace Kelley Art Foundation], Record Book no. 1.

78. Williamson to Ranney, Museum President, June 17, 1901; Minutes of the John Huntington Art and Polytechnic Trust, June 24, 1904, vol. 1. Having the same participants on all boards became policy. Edwin Perkins, however, resigned in 1911, citing conflict of interest, see Perkins to CMA, December 11, 1911, Cleveland Museum of Art [now the Horace Kelley Art Foundation], Record Book no. 2.

79. The land was transferred on January 13, 1900. Records of Deeds, 746: 258, Cuyahoga County.

80. Members of the building committee were Henry Ranney, president; J. M. Jones, J. H. Wade, vice presidents, who were *ex officio*, W. B. Sanders, L. E. Holden, and H. A. Kelley.

81. For the most complete surviving account of Kelley's estate, see "Probate Record of Horace Kelley," which contains the following four items: (1) "In the matter of the estate of Horace Kelley, Application for Probate of Will, filed December 11, 1890;" (2) "In re Estate of Horace Kelley, Report of Sale, filed April 15, 1893" [this reports the sale of two parcels of land lying between Michigan and Canal Streets and Canal Street and Lime Street to Thomas Woods for $11,000]; (3) "Estate of Horace Kelley, Second Partial Statement, filed January 2, 1894" [this reports total receipts as $48,924.48 and expenditures and fees of $41,602.77, leaving $7,321.71 cash on hand]; and (4) "In re Estate of Horace Kelley ... Final Account, filed January 22, 1900" [this reports a total cash flow through the estate of $135,180.05; while most of the money went for the payment of taxes, repairs on property, insurance premiums, Mrs. Kelley's annual annuity, and for the purchase of a monument to Horace Kelley, the Trustees paid themselves commissions on collections, and in November 1899 Ranney, Jones, and A. S. Kelley were paid "extra compensation" of $9,000]; Doc. 25, no. 4836, Probate Court Records, Cuyahoga County Archives.

82. J. G. W. Cowles, Hermon A. Kelley, and H. R. Hatch. Hermon Kelley was appointed agent of real estate at a salary of $50 per month to collect rents, arrange leases, etc. Minutes of the Board of Trustees of the Cleveland Museum of Art [now the Horace Kelley Art Foundation], January 31, 1901, Record Book no. 1. This continues an earlier arrangement he had with Kelley's estate.

83. Cleveland Museum of Art [now the Horace Kelley Art Foundation], Record Book no. 1. Jones, Sanders, Wade, and Kelley were at this meeting.

84. Exactly how many institutions they wrote to is not known, but at least one letter survives. Hermon A. Kelley to Museum of Fine Arts, Boston, asking for information, February 23, 1900, Dir.AC3, Cleveland Museum of Art, folder 1, Museum of Fine Arts, Boston, Archives.

85. Liberty Holden, "The Public Buildings of European Cities," typescript, Meeting of the Cleveland Chamber of Commerce, May 20, 1901, MS. 3471, Western Reserve Historical Society.

86. For an analysis of the Group Plan, see Walter C. Leedy, Jr., "Cleveland's Struggle for Self-Identity: Aesthetics, Economics and Politics," in Richard Guy Wilson and Sidney K. Robinson, eds., *Modern Architecture in America: Visions and Revisions* (Ames: Iowa State University Press, 1991), 75-105.

87. Paul Ells et al. to Trustees of the Historical Society of Cleveland, July 19, 1895, Minute Book, 1/M/1, Box 3, Archives, Western Reserve Historical Society.

88. Annual Meeting of the Western Reserve Historical Society, May 7, 1895, Minutes of Meetings, 1892-1908, 1/M/1, Box 3, Archives, Western Reserve Historical Society.

89. There were several major opinions: Samuel Williamson to Ranney, President, Cleveland Museum of Art, June 17,

1901, November 6, 1901; Judge James M. Jones, April 2, 1901; Hermon A. Kelley, October 17, 1901; William B. Sanders, February 19, 1903; and J. M. Henderson to E. R. Perkins, President, John Huntington Art and Polytechnic Trust, April 28, 1904, Kelly-Huntington file, Corporate, CMA Archives.

90. Kelley to Sanders, February 9, 1912, W. B. Sanders file, 1909-13, Harold T. Clark Papers, CMA Archives.

91. Edwin R. Perkins, President of the John Huntington Art and Polytechnic Trust, to the Cleveland Museum of Art [now the Horace Kelley Art Foundation], July 12, 1904. Approved at meeting, June 24, 1904. John Huntington Art and Poly-technic Trust, Minute Book, CMA Archives.

92. Hermon Kelley to Judge Williamson, October 17, 1901, content noted in Sanders to the Trustees of the John Hunt-ington Art and Polytechnic Trust, February 19, 1903, Kelley-Huntington file, Construction of Original Building, Corpo-rate, CMA Archives.

93. They added the phrase "for the purpose of securing the co-operation of other persons or corporations in the erection and maintenance of other institutions of the kind herein by granting or leasing them portions of its lands ... joining in them in the erection of buildings, joint use, and occupancy." Meeting of Members, May 6, 1905, and Meeting of the Board of Trustees, June 5, 1905, Cleveland Museum of Art [now the Horace Kelley Art Foundation], Record Book no. 1.

94. *Cleveland Plain Dealer*, June 25, 1905.

THE ARCHITECTS
RESPOND

Figure 5. Thought to be Liberty E. and Delia E. Holden's wedding portrait, 1860. Liberty Holden was one of the first to recognize the opportunities for real estate investment in the east end of Cleveland, just when the city was entering into a period of rapid growth and development. Connected with the many civic improvements (water, gas, education, etc.) required for a modern city, Holden served as the first Chairman of the Museum's Building Committee.

With money in hand and a functional solution that would permit the building of a single structure to house the museums called for by the three major bequests, the President of the Huntington Trust, E. R. Perkins, wasted no time in appointing a Building Committee of six. He named H. C. Ranney, W. B. Sanders, Charles W. Bingham, J. H. Wade, L. E. Holden (Figure 5), and H. A. Kelley to the committee on June 7, 1905. It had complete authority to secure architects and prepare the architectural plans.[1] The very next day this committee held its first meeting and elected Liberty Holden as chairman. The members decided to visit and interview the Trustees of the Albright Art Gallery in Buffalo (Figure 6) and other galleries in America and Europe to obtain information about selecting an architect and other matters. They did not, however, expect to choose an architect until fall.[2]

Afraid that the commission would go to a non-Clevelander, the local chapter of the American Institute of Architects held a special meeting on June 10, 1905—it was not customary for them to meet in the summer—at the office of Hubbell and Benes. They adopted a resolution urging that Cleveland architects be employed for important public buildings. A copy of the resolution was specifically sent to the Building Committee. To influence local sentiment, it was released for publication in the newspapers and was sent to the Cleveland Chamber of Commerce as well. Furthermore, a publicity campaign was planned and implemented.[3] By taking aggressive action, the architects hoped to reverse the trend toward employing outsiders which had been gaining momentum after the Group Plan commission of 1902. It was their belief that the best results could be obtained by the employment of home talent; the rationale was not only that Cleveland's architects were just as good, but that they could "handle the work infinitely better because of being right on the ground all the time and able to give close attention to the work."[4] Formal architectural education in the United States was then just

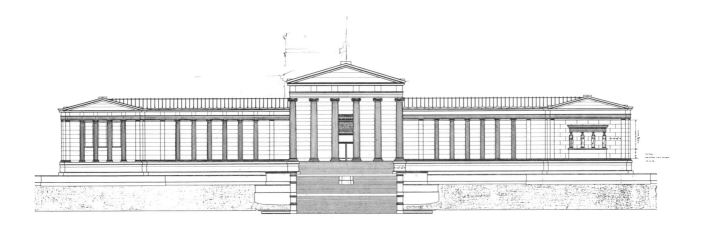

Figure 6. The Albright Art Gallery, Buffalo, New York (today, the Albright-Knox Art Gallery), is located in a park near Buffalo's public transportation system.

In 1905, when it opened, it was characterized as "the finest example of pure Greek architecture to be found in America."

emerging from its infancy, and Cleveland, like other midwestern cities, could attract and retain academically trained, high caliber architects.

The Building Committee was presumably aware, because of its research into galleries, that the Boston Museum of Fine Arts had used a similar, although more refined, rationale when choosing an architect. Samuel Warren of Boston instructed his building committee in 1902: "Hire a Boston architect.... Intimate relationship ... [and] civic pride will be a help and inspiration to the kind of man we are willing to employ.... Our museum ought to grow out of our own soil, and be the product of our own children."[5]

Toward the end of June, even before the Building Committee's studies were completed—it was not, of course, totally uninformed as it had the resource material collected by the first committee appointed in 1900—the *Cleveland Plain Dealer* reported that while nothing had been decided, even tacitly, it was the sentiment of the Building Committee that the gallery "will be of classic Greek architecture and that its lines will be severe and strong."[6] They took as their model the Albright Art Gallery in Buffalo, which had just opened in May 1905 to great national acclaim.

The committee met again in November to discuss the proper method of selecting an architect and determining the kind of structure to be built. While they took no action on these points, they decided to have a survey of the site prepared, and the committee members contemplated rounding out the oval and making changes in the parkways. To this end, they would work with the city's Director of Public Works, Daniel E. Leslie, and with City Council.[7]

Although the actual Building Committee minutes are silent as to the process of choosing an architect during the last months of 1905, the committee asked Edmund M. Wheelwright, who was the consulting architect for the new Boston Museum of Fine Arts, to give a presentation. For his visit, he had requested permission from Samuel Warren of Boston to borrow some resource material "to illustrate the talk ... which ... [Cleveland] asked me to give looking towards my

possible but not promised employment upon their work." Permission was granted, and Wheelwright came to Cleveland in early December 1905.[8] His talk is not recorded, but it is known that he exhibited plans and section drawings of European museums, eight albums of photographs, and a portfolio containing the competition for the Darmstadt Museum.[9] (At that time, German museums were considered to be in the avant garde with respect to museum design and exhibition practices.) He followed this up with two letters, dated December 13, 1905, and April 7, 1906. He apparently made a positive impression because Holden met him in New York to discuss securing his services as consulting architect.[10]

It is understandable that Cleveland's Building Committee focused on Wheelwright and Boston.[11] Since 1903 the Boston committee had systematically studied all aspects of museum design and arrangement, taking as scientific an approach as possible. They had traveled to Europe, taking extensive notes and collecting photographs on everything positive that they saw; they had even built an experimental gallery at their new site with movable walls and floor, so they could examine the arrangement and dimensions of exhibition rooms, lighting, heating, and ventilation. Their findings were summarized in a series of private reports to their Trustees. A typescript of one of their reports, "The Museum Commission in Europe," with a section written by Wheelwright, dated January 1905, reached the hands of Hermon Kelley.[12]

No doubt reacting to Wheelwright's visit in December, Cleveland's Building Committee met on January 6, 1906, to inspect proposals from certain architects that had been prepared on their own initiative; it was understood that the committee was under no obligation whatsoever.[13]

To help out, the Cleveland Chamber of Commerce reconstituted its Committee on the Art Gallery. At its first meeting on January 25, 1906, this committee heard a progress report and proffered its cooperation and assistance in any manner possible. The chairman of the committee, Homer H. Johnson, who was one of the most politically powerful men in the city, believed it desirable for the Chamber's president to mention the art museum in his annual address, and accordingly he invited Ranney and Hermon Kelley to speak before the committee in March 1906. While Ranney presented a short history of the undertaking, Kelley frankly suggested that the president should express satisfaction with the progress that had been made and that the committee work against the permanent placement of a new zoo at the location of the existing one—just north of the art gallery site. While Kelley saw the two institutions as incongruous, he had another objective in mind: the site of the present zoo should be reserved for future growth of the Museum.[14] In December 1906 Kelley himself petitioned City Council to remove the zoo from Wade Park, mentioning in addition to the above rationale that it would interfere with the architecture and landscaping of the Museum.[15] Decorum demanded that a suitable setting be created. In 1907 city officials voted to move the zoological collections to Brookside Park near West 25th Street.

By May 1906 almost a year had passed and the committee had yet to select an architect. As a result, the City Clerk inquired as to when the Museum would be completed.[16] Finding Liberty Holden's response[17] inadequate, City Councilman Henry Pears submitted a resolution requesting information as to what power, if any, the city had to compel the Building Committee to proceed more quickly.[18] City Solicitor Newton Baker reported to council that the city had no authority over the Museum plans, but that since the Trusts were governed by the laws of the State of Ohio, the Attorney General had ample power to begin proceedings to oust the present Trustees and to substitute new ones. And, if this was council's wish, they should pass a resolution asking the Attorney General to take action. He counseled against it, however, since the court would grant so extreme a remedy only when it was plainly necessary, and at this time Liberty Holden said the committee was about to select an architect.[19] Complaints about the slowness of

the Trustees' progress were not new, but in the years to come public anger would grow.

At the annual dinner of the Cleveland Chamber of Commerce held in June 1906, Johnson defended the committee's painstaking pace and advocated greater civic interest in the project. He set forth the idea that an art gallery is more than just a stone structure and needed to be coupled with an organization that could present the collection most effectively for public education and culture. He requested every Clevelander to deliberate on such questions as: What character shall our art museum have? Shall its collection be specialized in hopes of excelling in some line? Should the objects collected be primarily for people's pleasure? Or should works of historical importance be included, thus teaching the principles of the history of art? If so, should they be displayed in a separate department, open only to students? Should the museum reach out to the masses, possibly by including a library, a lecture hall, and galleries for temporary exhibitions? Should examples of arts and crafts be included? Should cooperation be sought with other educational institutions in the city? Johnson's admonition was not only aimed at enlightening Cleveland's decision-makers about art opportunities but also at the Building Committee: "I know they appreciate the public nature of their office and would welcome the co-operation of the public."[20]

Over the next year the Chamber's art gallery committee sought to help the Trustees in developing a program for the future museum. In October 1906 they invited Kenyon Cox, a New York artist-critic who had worked for Wade in Cleveland, to speak on a public policy for an art gallery in America. Believing it impossible to build a first-rate European collection because of the high cost of art and tariffs, Cox suggested collecting contemporary American art, for the benefit of future generations. Of greater interest, he advocated building a museum of documents—photographic reproductions of paintings and plaster casts of sculptures—for the critical study of art. A museum built along these lines would be designed

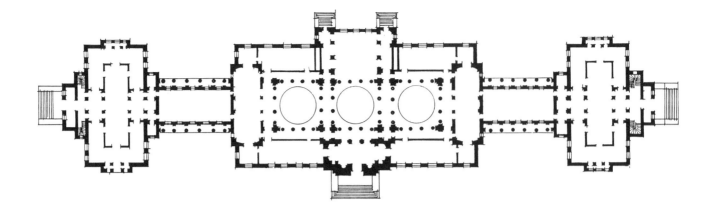

Figure 7. The initial idea for the Cleveland Museum was to build three separately owned galleries that would look like one large museum while giving visual recog- nition to the three estates that were re- sponsible for it.
    The architects adapt- ed the time-honored model of the Palladian villa with flanking end pavilions. Proposal, July 2, 1906, Hubbell and Benes, Cleveland Mu- seum of Art.

more like a library with stacks and would have only a small exhibition area where casual visitors could get a rapid bird's-eye view of the whole history of art by looking at a selection of photographs.[21]

To the same end, in the following year the Chamber's gallery committee held a private conference that included several Museum Trustees, the President of the Board of Education, the Superintendent of Schools, and Sir Caspar Purdon Clarke, Director of the Metropolitan Museum of Art in New York and former Director of the South Kensington Museum (now the Victoria and Albert Museum), London.[22] While it is impossible to evaluate the impact of these efforts, the Trustees did recognize that they needed professional assistance.

The Building Committee did not evolve a systematic approach, as did other museums, for choosing an architect, and as far as it is known, they never contemplated having a formal architectural competition to select one, as was then commonplace for publicly owned museums. In early June 1906 the committee visited the office of J. Milton Dyer, examined drawings that he had voluntarily prepared, and listened to his suggestions. By the end of June 1906 it was the sense of the committee that if a local architect or architects were selected, Wheelwright should be employed as a consulting architect or as counsel to the committee.[23] Clearly, they felt that his experience in thinking through what a museum is on both the functional and the constructive levels—something no local firm could claim to have done—would ensure success. Although the Building Committee continued to show interest in Dyer, they decided on June 29, 1906, to invite Hubbell and Benes to display drawings that had also been voluntarily done in hopes of winning the commission. They reexamined Dyer's proposal along with that of Hubbell and Benes on July 3, 1906.

Although nothing is recorded about the appearance of Dyer's proposal,[24] judging from the other public work that his office was doing at the time, he would have favored a Francophile classicism style.[25] A graduate of the Ecole des Beaux-Arts in Paris, Dyer was already a noted designer. Earlier, he had won the much-coveted commission for designing Cleveland's new City Hall.

Hubbell and Benes's drawing of July 2, 1906, however, is preserved (Figure 7). The firm proposed a unified building consisting of three distinct parts. The major part was a center pavilion with its longest axis running as parallel as possible to East Boulevard. Joined to this center section by means of galleries were two end pavilions, with their longest axes running perpendicular to East Boulevard. Internally, Hubbell conceived of the central and visually most important section as a series of three axially aligned, domed, major spaces[26] around which was an open, colonnaded corridor. Off this corridor was a series of rectangular galleries. Such a design gave visual symbolization to each of the three Trusts and could be built in units, as the money from each estate became available. In making their presentation, Hubbell and Benes placed their proposal on the same sheet with the plans of other museums drawn to the same scale, thereby providing the committee with a visual frame of reference. In creating their design, they had studied the sizes, proportions, construction materials, and architectural styles of other galleries.[27]

It is not recorded how the Trustees reacted to either Dyer's or Hubbell's proposal, but they decided to defer making a decision on the selection of the architect until Kelley returned from Europe. Three weeks later, they decided to again postpone a decision until the services of Wheelwright were secured as consulting architect, "giving him full discretionary authority in the premises...."[28] This most unusual stipulation warrants an explanation.

For the final design of the Boston museum Samuel Warren had proposed that Wheelwright and R. Clipston Sturgis work together, with Wheelwright as senior architect; but Sturgis demanded equality and was not willing to take a subordinate position. He recognized Wheelwright's superiority in matters of the composition of masses and of design, while he had

abilities in the logical use of data, etc.[29] With the idea that Sturgis would be given the commission for Boston, Wheelwright drew up the terms under which he would serve as consulting architect: "The consulting architect is to control the plans, the Architect is to control the exterior and interior design.... The design and construction of the building is to have the final approval of the Consulting Architect." Warren offered Wheelwright a contract as consulting architect, but under other conditions, in January 1906. Wheelwright declined because he "would have little influence over the development of the work, while ... [he] ... would not be relieved from responsibility for its outcome."[30] (The commission for Boston eventually went to Guy Lowell.) In all likelihood then it was Wheelwright, himself, who insisted on having real decision-making authority in negotiations with Cleveland's Building Committee. This authority, combined with the committee's confidence in him, had major consequences.

By July 25, 1906, Liberty Holden had made a contract with Wheelwright, and he hoped that the committee would take final action in the selection of local architects at a meeting scheduled for July 30.[31] No decision, however, was made. In preparation for the next meeting on September 4, 1906, Holden employed a successful stratagem: he asked every member to express in writing three persons or firms of architects in order of their preference. After an informal discussion, J. H. Wade finally moved, and it was carried, that Hubbell and Benes (Figures 8 and 9) be selected as architects, subject to the supervision and cooperation of Wheelwright. This decision was applauded in the architectural press.[32]

While it is not known how many architects were actually considered, it was no surprise that Hubbell and Benes were chosen, for W. Dominick Benes was known by his contemporary colleagues as J. H. Wade's personal architect. Before Benes's partnership with Hubbell, he had designed the interiors for the Wade yacht, the *Wadena* (1890), and the music room in Wade's home at East 40th and Euclid Avenue.[33]

Figure 8. Benjamin S. Hubbell (1867-1953). Born in Leavenworth, Kansas, he received his B.S. and M.S. in architecture (1894) from Cornell University. A member of the Masons, Cleveland Chamber of Commerce, American Institute of Architects, and the Colonial Club, Hubbell was a leading advocate for the development of University Circle.

Figure 9. W. Dominick Benes (1857-1935). Born in Prague, Bohemia, Benes immigrated to Cleveland in 1867. He left school at the age of 15 to study architecture with his uncle, John V. Benes, in Chicago. First apprenticed (1873-1876) with Cleveland architect Andrew Mitermiler, Benes next joined the firm of Coburn and Barnum, which later became the firm of Hubbell and Benes.

And, during the time that both Hubbell and Benes were briefly in partnership with Coburn and Barnum (1896), that firm was given the commission to design the new home for the Western Reserve Historical Society, a project for which Wade donated a mosaic floor and played a major role on the building committee.[34] After Hubbell and Benes formed their own partnership in 1897, several Wade commissions followed: the Wade Memorial Chapel (1899) in Lake View Cemetery, the Citizens' Savings and Trust Company Building (1903), and after the Museum commission was let, the Wade residence and farm building at Thomasville, Georgia. Furthermore, Hubbell and Benes were commissioned in 1904 to design the nearby Cleveland School of Art (Wade had not only donated the land for the school but had served on their planning committee).[35] Wade's influence swayed the committee in favor of Hubbell and Benes, which was emerging as one of Cleveland's most aggressive, larger, and more diverse architectural firms. A year earlier, in 1905, for example, the firm had won the commission to design the city's new West Side Market House.[36]

Even without a contract, the architects set to work immediately developing their original presentation with the understanding that the museum building should be a monumental structure expressing both internally and externally the tri-party agreement.[37] By December 1906 committee members were viewing preliminary plans. During this early stage, Hubbell and Benes naively thought they could give free reign to their fancy and design a beautiful classical building unimpeded by the cost or practical concerns that "usually handicap an Architect's efforts in such a manner as to make the result that he produces far below the standard of his desire."[38] They sought to design a museum with a picturesque outline and pleasing proportions, one that would in fact be a work of art in itself.[39] Wheelwright's approach to museum design defined the problem quite differently: "We premise that the practical needs of the museum are to be the main consideration in the problem; the external effect is subordinate.... Architectural expression will come later ... program first."[40]

Wheelwright submitted a detailed report to the Building Committee in which he made several important recommendations that were to guide the initial design decision-making process. He advocated top-lighted galleries to increase hanging space and to give important works a "dignity of axial position." In such galleries doorways could be positioned as needed and large crowds could be accommodated. By contrast, in side-lighted galleries windows take up valuable wall space and doorways need to be close to the window wall—to avoid glaring light. Thus, axial position could not be given to important works, and congestion was a common problem. Furthermore, he realized that to secure proper light on the pictures hung near the back walls, it might be necessary to bevel the side walls as a whole or in part to equalize the light.

Besides technical observations, Wheelwright thought about the psychological impact of different gallery types on observers. In side-lighted galleries he felt, for example, that pictures benefit as individual works more than in their association with other pictures, and that the observer feels himself more intensely associated with the artist's work than if it were displayed under unusual or more formal conditions of top-lighted galleries. Sculpture, he recommended, should be placed in top-lighted galleries. He further advocated the association of furniture and other works of art with paintings. And because of an awareness of the history of museum architecture, he appreciated that until the eighteenth century no paintings had been hung in top-lighted galleries and therefore acknowledged the importance of side-lighted galleries for the exhibition of important older pictures.[41]

In May 1907 the architects were finally given a budget: one million dollars.[42] Not solely the result of programmatic requirements, this figure was set high enough to secure the investment in a single building of a suitable proportion of the funds from each of the three estates to make any future withdrawal from the tripartite arrangement impossible.[43]

During the design process, the architects considered the plans for the building itself separately from its context. The most pressing artistic and functional problem, they soon determined, was that of the site (Figure 10). The lot with its primary side fronting on East Boulevard did not orient itself to any important view (one end or corner of any proposed building would be presented to the artificial lake located in Wade Park and to Euclid Avenue, which was also the city's main thoroughfare). Also, it was not large enough to provide an adequate driveway to the main entrance, was not generous enough to allow for a satisfactory foreground in the park, was poorly oriented (north-south) in terms of affording good natural light, and did not allow for possible future expansion. The major thrust during this early design stage was to create a "dignified approach" and a formal setting for the proposed monumental structure: the ritual of arrival and the Museum's image in the urban context were considered as important as the design of the building itself. Wheelwright's constant criticism was instrumental at this stage of the design process.[44]

The architects made several proposals to resolve these problems. One was to open a new street through the Excelsior Club property (built in 1908, the Club building is now Thwing Hall of Case Western Reserve University) thus intersecting with Bellflower Road from which point it was to be extended to the main entrance, which was to be located on the east side of the building. The residents of Bellflower Road objected to this proposal, however, and the cost for municipal improvements was too great.[45] Another proposal called for a new street through the Brunner property (which was located west of the Excelsior Club parcel on Euclid Avenue), making a curve on its westerly end similar to that on Bellflower Road. By this treatment, an open park space was provided on the easterly front of the building. This plan was rejected by the Building Committee as inadequate. Yet another plan suggested opening a new road from East 105th Street. It seemed that the ideal solution would never be found.

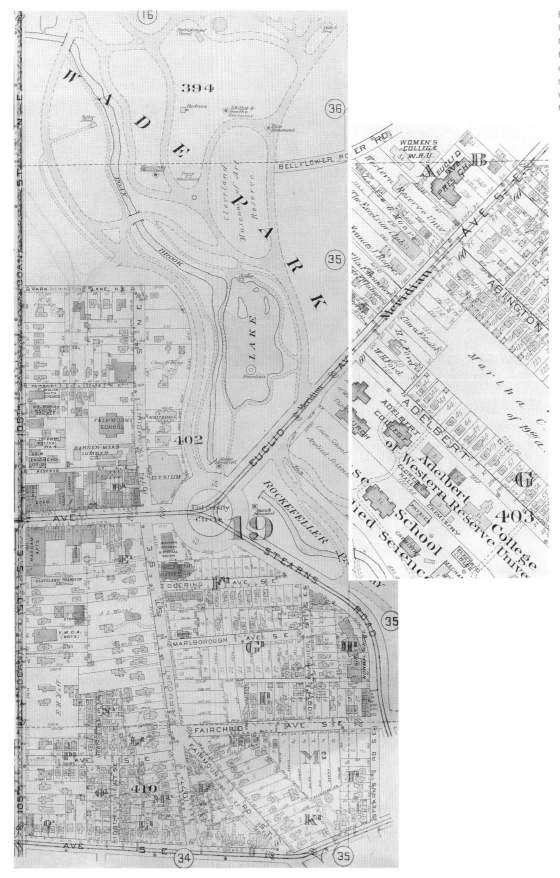

Figure 10. Plan of the University Circle area, Cleveland, showing the location and size of the original Museum site before land was exchanged with the city.

Paralleling their efforts to develop the site plan, by July 1907 the architects had studied at least fourteen schemes, each with many variants, for the building itself (Figures 11 and 12). They took into consideration how people move through galleries (Figure 13), the height of gallery ceilings, and the locations of lighting sources, both natural and artificial. They were aware of "museum fatigue"—the result of the physical effort of walking and standing in combination with emotional and mental concentration. They considered museum fatigue to be related to the sheer number of objects viewed (Wheelwright selected 600 paintings as a maximum besides those shown in temporary galleries)[46] rather than to the exhibition of art that was "irrelevant" to the socio-economic makeup of the population, as did some of their contemporaries.[47] They studied how objects should be viewed—whether on axis, etc. A symbiotic relationship developed between the solution of aesthetic and practical problems, and each successive scheme became more compact. In the end, the architects presented four distinct proposals for critical consideration. The Building Committee dismissed one scheme straightaway because the internal arrangement lacked perfect symmetry in plan and would therefore produce a "less pleasing effect." A second was eliminated because a one-story building would be less economical and effective. The third was discarded because it was unquestionably over budget. The committee instructed the architects to develop the fourth scheme by making the portico wider at the main entrance. To make it easier to understand, the architects were instructed to produce a perspective rendering of it, along with first and second floor plans to a scale of 40 feet to the inch, and front and side elevations at a scale of 16 feet to the inch. Clearly, the committee was fundamentally concerned with the image of the building.

These drawings were presented to the Huntington Trustees on July 16, 1907. Although no contract had yet been signed with the architects, Holden, Kelley, and C. W. Fuller (the secretary to the Building Committee) arrived at a satisfactory agreement, and the committee finally approved a contract with Hubbell and Benes at their meeting. Still unsure, the committee members studied two different schemes with reference to the projected cost and the space available to each of the separate estates for exhibition purposes. Wheelwright cautioned that the effective display area would be less because of inadequate lighting. The committee members instructed him to submit the two different schemes to Edward Robinson,[48] who was then Assistant Director of the Metropolitan Museum in New York, for his critical comment (Figure 14). The plan favored by the committee was projected to be over budget.

At Wheelwright's insistence, Hubbell and Benes developed a radical new site plan by August 20, 1907; they changed the orientation of the building from north-south to east-west, with the main facade facing south toward Euclid Avenue. Wheelwright argued that the proper lighting of exhibition areas required that the building's longer axis be located in an east-west direction. That orientation would achieve a maximum of north light and avoid as far as possible shadows cast upon the skylights and windows from the higher parts of the building. Hubbell accepted this rationale and later articulated one other advantage: "a southern exposure best displays the beauties of a facade."[49] If accepted, however, this proposal would mandate a new site.

Nevertheless, it was the sense of the committee that because the proposed change of site would involve an exchange of land with the city, the project would be seriously delayed. So regardless of Wheelwright's protestations, the committee voted to proceed with a building on the original site, conditioned by the Huntington Trustees' agreement to pay for its portion of the building which was in excess of $500,000. They also instructed the architects to secure bids from Garet of Washington and Klee Brothers of New York to fabricate a plaster, 1/8-inch-scale model. On August 21, 1907, Holden, acting on his own initiative, instructed Hubbell by telephone to have the necessary trees removed and to have the engineer set stakes

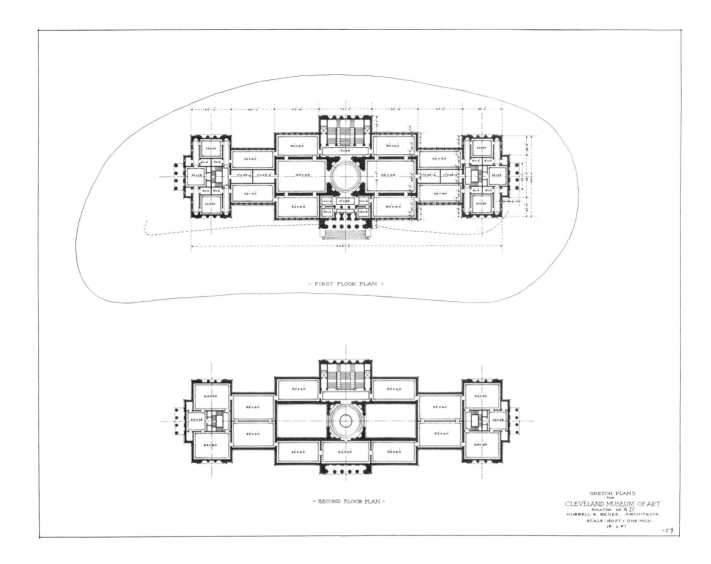

- FIRST FLOOR PLAN -

- SECOND FLOOR PLAN -

SKETCH PLANS
FOR
CLEVELAND MUSEUM OF ART
SOLUTION NO. 8.D
HUBBELL & BENES · ARCHITECTS
SCALE: 40 FT = ONE INCH.
10-2-07

Figures 11 and 12. Surviving proposals from about 1907 for the Museum parallel a proposal for the Administration Building, University of Cleveland, dating to about 1918. Note that the second story has skylights rather than windows. Plan, proposal no. 8D, Hubbell and Benes, Cleveland Museum of Art; rendering, signed October 2, 1907, Hubbell and Benes.

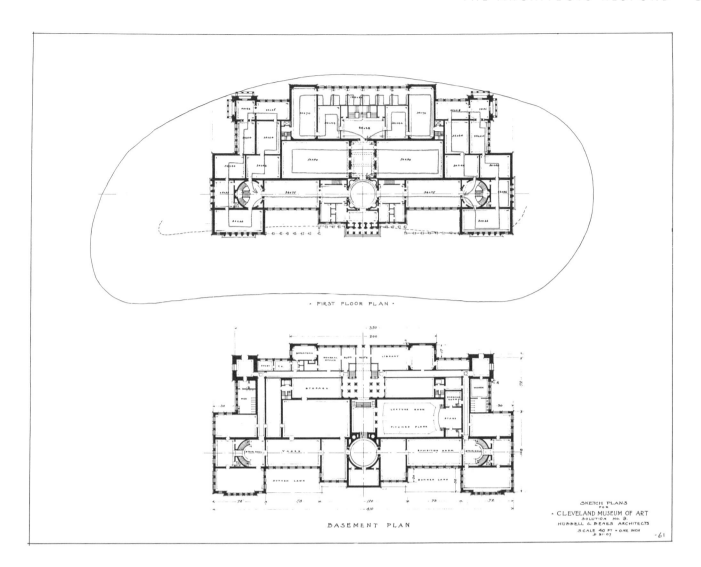

· FIRST FLOOR PLAN ·

BASEMENT PLAN

SKETCH PLANS
FOR
· CLEVELAND MUSEUM OF ART
SOLUTION No. 9.
HUBBELL & BENES ARCHITECTS
SCALE 40 FT = ONE INCH
5·31·07
-61

Figure 13. The Building Committee traced potential pathways through the galleries during the design process. Proposal no. 9, May 31, 1907, Hubbell and Benes, Cleveland Museum of Art. Tracings have been redrawn to ensure their visibility here.

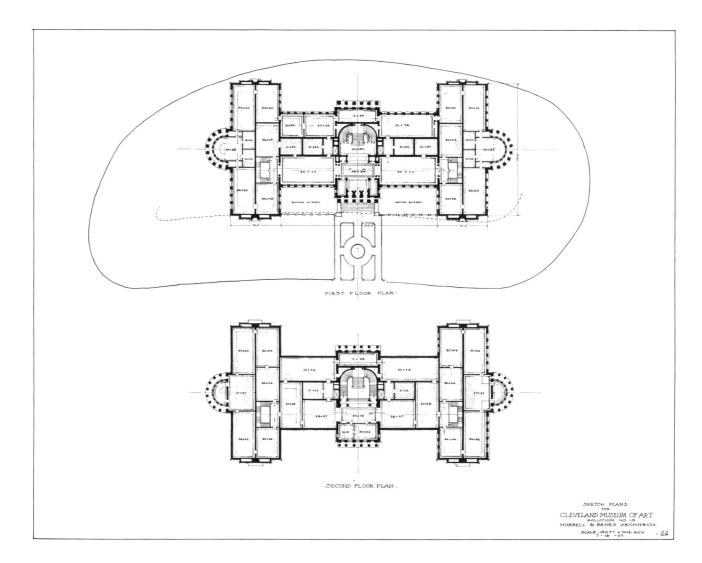

Figure 14. This was one of two schemes submitted to Edward Robinson, Assistant Director of the Metropolitan Museum in New York, for criticism. Proposal no. 13, July 16, 1907, Hubbell and Benes, Cleveland Museum of Art.

for locating the building and to do the necessary work to establish grades and approaches. Shortly thereafter, however, this site was rejected.

During the latter months of 1907, the committee decided to review their recommendation. The exact impetus for this action is not recorded, but in all likelihood it responded to the architects' persistent nagging for an east-west oriented building to be located on axis with an extension of Adelbert Road (Figure 15). This proposed extension would form a new eastern boundary for Wade Park. The suggested new site was located 800 feet north of Euclid Avenue, and restrictions would be imposed to keep any dwellings built on the easterly side of Adelbert Road far enough back from the street line to allow the entire front façade of the Art Museum building to be seen from Euclid Avenue. The building would thus be visually integrated into the main life of the city.[50] To this end, both the committee and architects met with Mayor Tom L. Johnson, Director William J. Springborn, Director Daniel E. Leslie, and the Chief Engineer of the city's Park Department, William Stinchcomb. As the proposal required the purchase of a plot of land in the Wade allotment (now part of the Severance Hall site), with a frontage of about 350 feet on Euclid Avenue and a depth of 400 feet, Holden, Kelley, and

Figure 15. This rendering by Frederick C. Gottwald, of about 1908, evidently depicts the proposed museum located at the end of a hypothetical extension of Adelbert Road. At this time plans called for two main exhibition floors with the upper floor lighted by means of skylights.

Bingham were authorized to negotiate with J. H. Wade for additional land[51] to be purchased by the city. Based on Hubbell's presentation, Mayor Johnson approved this conception and agreed to cooperate with the committee, as the new site required an exchange of land with the city. There was, however, the question of the city's capability of paying an estimated $90,000 for the additional land on Euclid Avenue needed for the street and park extension. Under a verbal agreement, the Trustees were responsible for paying the hefty sum of $229,000 for site improvements (building a new park entrance, grading and filling in the site, and constructing a number of new approach roads).[52] In June 1908 the plan was approved by both the Kelley Foundation and the Huntington Trust, and the order given to proceed with the working drawings for the building. The architects were further instructed to include a sub-basement for the mechanical plant and to get separate bids for using granite, limestone, or sandstone for the exterior.[53] At that time, the Huntington Trust was ready to proceed with the erection of the building as soon as they were in legal possession of the site.

By August 1908 this proposed location had to be rejected because of its cost to the city:[54] Cleveland's voters were not disposed to pass bond elections for any purpose whatsoever during Mayor Tom L. Johnson's administration. The realization of the desirability of an east-west oriented building, however, was now so strongly imbedded that a new, but different solution was sought.

In concert with city officials, by December 2, 1908, a new plan had been developed for the building to face University Circle and the Wade Park lake. To minimize the costs of site preparation, the building was to be located on level ground close to Bellflower Road. This solution was suggested in a letter written in late 1907 to Mayor Johnson by Rabbi Moses J. Gries of The Temple, as a better alternative to the Adelbert Road plan: "there could be no more attractive sight [sic] for the new Art Museum than a site overlooking the lake in Wade Park, and a building that would be in commanding view as one looked across the lake."[55] It probably will never be known if this was mere coincidence or if the Rabbi's suggestion stimulated consideration of this site, but it is known that the park engineer (Stinchcomb) had first suggested this location to the Trustees. Up to this time, the architects' preferred solution had been an axial pedestrian-vehicle approach to the building, in concert with the popular Beaux-Arts planning principles of the day, which emphasized a highly ordered scheme and movement of the user through it—architecture experienced aesthetically. When people approached it, the building would offer a commanding, although static, impression. By contrast, with the Wade Park lake in front of it, people could still see the complete structure and therefore subliminally understand its importance in urban culture, as in the Adelbert Road plan. However, they would be forced to approach the Museum obliquely, much like the Parthenon in Athens, thus seeing the building as a delightful series of changing images. This radical new conception, which influenced all future decisions, was adopted after receiving consulting architect Wheelwright's approval.[56]

At first, to provide a sufficiently long east-west frontage, enlarging the plot by purchasing land located to the east was proposed. However, this proved to be too expensive ($180,000 for the city for land, and $101,000 for the Trustees for improving the site and relocating the approach roads). Thereafter, Mayor Johnson suggested to Stinchcomb that the Museum's land be widened on its westerly side out of park lands, and a plan for exchanging land not actually required for the Museum's building itself for the land to the west was drawn up by the park engineer. Once this idea caught on, the architects, Trustees, and city officials debated exactly where the east-west axis of the building should be located. The architects fought for a location north of Bellflower Road. Some city officials wanted to maintain that area as park land; located south of the zoo, it was the only level playing ground in the park and was finely forested.

With due respect to other city officials, Mayor Johnson made the decision to proceed with the architects' desired location.[57]

The factors actually determining the precise location of the building were: (1) an adequate approach, (2) good orientation for providing natural light to the galleries, (3) a sufficient distance (75 feet) from East Boulevard, which was required by the deed restriction, (4) capacity for potential expansion to the north, (5) the cost of excavation, and (6) an adjacent location to provide a convenient place for depositing the earth removed during construction. The committee was so well satisfied with this solution that they hoped that the project could be put in definite shape in the next few months.[58]

Because the city owned the land in front of the projected museum, Stinchcomb worked out the landscaping plan. He proposed building a lagoon just north of the existing artificial lake and, beyond it, a formal garden, through which the Museum would be approached. Broad winding stairways were proposed to lead down from the Museum to the garden and from there down to the water's edge, where a boat house and shelter house, harmonizing in design with the museum, would be erected. To reach the Wade Park lake, boats would pass under an arched bridge of picturesque design which would be one of the striking features of the approach as viewed from Euclid Avenue.[59] A perspective rendering of the proposed solution by Frederick C. Gottwald was published in the *Cleveland Plain Dealer* with the caption "terrace will carry out old world effect" (Figure 16).[60] In order to achieve this plan, an exchange of land with the city was necessary. As this appeared to be perfunctory, the architects were given the go-ahead on December 2, 1908, to proceed with the working drawings and to have cost estimates made for the building. Furthermore, a committee consisting of Sanders, Hubbell, and Kelley was empowered to submit the latest proposition to the city.[61]

A public announcement was made that construction would begin in the spring and that the building materials would probably be granite. This decree was made not by the committee, but by Liberty Holden and was published in his paper, the *Cleveland Plain Dealer*, on December 19, 1908.[62] Upon reading this, the children and grandchildren of the late John Huntington immediately demanded that the Museum be built out of stone supplied by the Cleveland Stone Company. Huntington had acquired two-fifths of the capital stock in this company before his death, and the dividends were still providing income to the estate and therefore to the art trust. His heirs wrote to the Huntington Trustees: "we know that he could not have entertained for a moment the suggestions of expending his charity in the erection of an Art Museum out of material other than material of his company."[63] The question of the type of stone used for Cleveland's public buildings, however, went well beyond the desires of the Huntington heirs. It had first became a major public issue in 1902, when the Federal Building was being planned for downtown Cleveland and continued throughout the decade. The decision about what stone should be used for the Museum's superstructure was resolved much later, in 1913, after construction actually commenced.

Because the Park Department's plan presented no opportunity for an economical disposition of 29,000 cubic feet of excavated material, during the early months of 1909 the committee had a modified site plan and cost estimates prepared by the F. A. Pease Engineering Company. The variant plan projected a savings of $11,000.[64] Based on this data, Wheelwright wrote a proposed memorandum of agreement between the City and the Kelley Foundation for the necessary trade of park land for the proposed new site.[65] The agreement also articulated who would bear the cost of landscaping and park improvements (the Museum was prepared to donate the fill material for the long contemplated 500-foot-long culvert over Doan Creek and pay an additional $15,000 toward its cost). The covered culvert was to be landscaped over.[66] After negotiations began with the city, Pease's plan was rejected in favor of the city's own, which called for the enlargement of the lake in front of the Museum. Since the city had no capital to pay for this, however, the administration proposed that the Museum pay for it and for the construction of the Doan culvert in a new location. The city viewed these projects as essential to the improvement of Wade Park. The Museum proposed that the exchange of land not be equal, acre for acre, but requested an additional one and one-half acres, to remain at present park land, and be reserved for future use for a Museum addition. Since the Museum was proposing that the city hand over more land than it would receive in return, Democratic Mayor Johnson wanted it stipulated in the deed that the Museum would be open free to the public on certain days, an idea he may have gotten from City Solicitor Baker.[67]

In an August 1909 behind-closed-doors interview, Mayor Johnson, along with Baker and Leslie, indicated to the Trustees that they would recommend to City Council, and use their influence to secure approval of, the exchange of lands if the Museum would pay $65,000 toward the improvement, coupled with a requirement that the Museum be open free on all Saturdays and public holidays from 10 a.m. to 5 p.m. and on Sundays from 2 p.m. to 5 p.m. for eleven

Figure 16. Newspaper sketch of Frederick C. Gottwald's rendering of the proposed Cleveland Museum of Art if located facing the Wade Park lake.

months of the year.[68] The Trustees immediately put out a press release stating that Huntington provided for free days in his will which they were bound to honor, but since they did not know what the future might hold, they would not enter into a contractually binding agreement for definite free days. (Today Cleveland remains one of the few major museums in the world that does not charge an admission fee or request a specified donation.) Privately, they communicated with Johnson and Baker, agreeing to pay the requested $65,000 but proposing that the specific free day stipulation apply only to the possible future extension of the Museum on the additional one and one-half acres. On September 1, 1909, Mayor Johnson said he would withdraw his demand for free days, if the Trustees would agree to a foot-for-foot even trade, which would enable them to construct the first building. The Trustees, however, continued to demand the additional land for a future expansion.[69] In response, on September 9, Baker indicated that the free days must apply to the entire building and, in a conciliatory approach, indicated that Johnson would agree to a lesser dollar amount if a mutual agreement with the city on economies could be effected.[70] Negotiations continued into the beginning of December when the committee broke them off.[71] Because of ill health, Wheelwright was now out of the picture. For his contribution he was paid $7,327.99 for the years 1907 through 1909.[72] Hubbell later countered arguments made by the Building Committee about the size of his fees by noting that for architectural work done on a time basis, Wheelwright charged four times the amount actually paid to Wheelwright's office force.[73]

Looking to the future, the committee canceled negotiations with the city.[74] Johnson was ill at the time and had just lost the mayoral election to the Republican Herman C. Baehr, who was to assume office on January 1, 1910. Baker, however, was reelected as City Solicitor, although the new Republican Council immediately banned the Democrat from its meetings. Nonetheless, Baker continued to work toward solving the impasse and was largely responsible for the eventual settlement.[75]

By the end of January 1910 Mayor Baehr had met with the Trustees, viewed the plans, visited the site, and written to Kelley offering to facilitate a final agreement. Suffering continual public criticism for the construction delays—it had now been twenty years since Horace Kelley's death—Hermon Kelley struck back and placed the blame squarely on the "unbusinesslike and uncalled for bickering emanating from the city hall" (during the previous administration). He questioned Johnson's motives by quoting him as saying, "What I want is to be able to say to the people of Cleveland that I have secured the opening of the gallery free to them on certain days."[76] There was more propaganda value in this statement than reality: it was decisively rebutted in a long statement by Baker published in the *Cleveland Plain Dealer*.[77]

To quiet festering public criticism, in early February 1910, Liberty E. Holden announced that the contract for the building would be awarded in September with a completion date of September 1912.[78] At this time, however, no written agreement with the city had been reached.

By the end of February Mayor Baehr only wanted verbal assurance from the Trustees that the public would be given as many free Sundays, Saturdays, and holidays as possible.[79] However, the decision was City Council's to make, not his. In March the Mayor wrote to Council requesting that the Building Committee and the architects be allowed to appear to explain the land exchange.[80] Baehr then attended a meeting with the Museum's Building Committee in which he expressed his support based on their assurance that they were ready to proceed with the building.[81] Later, he inspected the site, accompanied by Andrew B. Lea, Director of Public Services, and City Engineer Robert Hoffman, and it was expected that an enabling ordinance would be introduced and rapidly passed.[82] Once introduced, on March 21, 1910, it was referred to the committees on Parks, City Property, and Judiciary, and to the City Solicitor;[83]

Council also planned to hold a public meeting on the subject. Trying to act in the public interest, Council questioned the objectives of these men of means.

When the Building Committee realized that an impasse still existed—Councilman Anton B. Sprosty, Chairman of the Committee on Parks, was in favor of placing stipulations in the deed relating to the number of free days[84]—it changed its request. Now, it asked merely for an equal exchange of land.[85] The members also informed Mayor Baehr that an expected shortfall in the Hurlbut estate reduced the building fund by 25 percent and, as a result, that a material change of plans might be necessary. Hedging their bets, they indicated that a building in the "Greek style of the one-story type" would be an even greater ornament to Wade Park than the "two-story Renaissance building" the city was anticipating.[86]

In late January 1910 the Hurlbut Trustees unexpectedly withdrew their commitment to erecting part of the building, because of insufficient funds.[87] This came as a blow. No one connected with the Museum project apparently knew the value of Hurlbut's estate prior to Mrs. Hurlbut's death on January 21, 1910. No explanation was offered for the shortfall, but the following reasons were suggested: (1) the value of Hurlbut's estate was overstated for effect in 1884 (no inventory had been filed with probate court), (2) as executrix, Mrs. Hurlbut may have made poor investments, (3) she may have spent part of the principal, which she was entitled to do under terms of the will, "to suitably support and maintain her in the station in life and position in society which she ... occupies," or (4) she may have given part of the principal away.[88] The attorney for the representatives of the estate, A. T. Hills, however, claimed that the $500,000 entertained by Museum authorities was the result of a miscalculation and that the entire estate probably never amounted to that much.[89] Nevertheless, in addition to the Hurlbut collection of works of art, the estate, valued at between $75,000 and $100,000, was sufficient to set up an operating and small purchase fund.[90] The Hurlbut Trustees were, of course, obli-

gated to pay $10,000 in architectural fees to Hubbell and Benes, which they did.[91]

In the aftermath of the shock, and without serious consideration, the Huntington Trust immediately agreed to pay two-thirds, and the Kelley Foundation one-third toward the cost of the future building, whatever the amount would be.[92] In spite of this, rumors floated around the city that the plans and the style of the building would have to be changed radically,[93] creating a crisis of confidence in the project.

Recognizing the implications of the fiscal shortfall, some Councilmen immediately demanded a guarantee that the building would cost at least $500,000, that construction would commence within six months, and that the completion date be stated (Figure 17). Newton Baker pressed well into April for similar stipulations,[94] but the Trustees steadfastly refused and issued an ultimatum. They would either let the project rest until a suitable trade could be made or erect a building on the site as it was. This second alternative, they declared, would be a calamity, because the building would not be properly placed.[95] By the middle of June 1910 Kelley wrote to the Council asking for an even foot-for-foot exchange of land without stipulations.[96] This action stimulated further

Figure 17. City officials continually inspected the proposed new site during 1909 and 1910. Newspaper clipping, July 24, 1910: Councilmen Burke, Bernstein, Hanratty, and Shimmon, and architect B. S. Hubbell (top row); Councilmen Fleming, White, and Horner (bottom row), and Museum representative Kelley.

discussion, another visit to the site by Council on July 1, 1910,[97] and finally a behind-closed-doors meeting of all the Council's committees, Baker, and the Trustees on July 8, at which a deal was struck (the Trustees were to pay for the relocation of statues, etc., then located in Wade Park, which did not conform to the new site plan).[98] Thereafter, a substitute ordinance was introduced and passed by Council on July 11, 1910, without the great debate expected by the public.[99] The Trustees had ostensibly promised that there would be certain "free days" each week.[100] The formal exchange of deeds followed later.

To provide ground space for future expansion, Kelley Foundation officials asked for and received from J. H. Wade a quitclaim deed for his reversionary rights for a 400-by-600-foot parcel of park land contiguous with the north side of the site, which they could request from the city twenty or thirty years in the future.

The building they expected to construct contained two stories of galleries, besides a ground floor in which the offices and an assembly room were to be located (Figure 18). The galleries on each floor would flow off domed rotundas—concessions to pure grandeur—whose purpose was to guide visitors without confusion or crowding. Two substantial, 85-by-46 foot, skylighted, two-story exhibition courts were to be located on the major axis of the building in which would be placed plaster casts of works from classical antiquity to the Renaissance. Around these courts, on both the first and second floors, would be a series of smaller exhibition rooms. Those on the south side would be skylighted on the second floor, while those on the first floor south, and on both floors north, would be side-lighted through windows. The primary entrance would be on the south side, facing the lake; there would be a basement for mechanical equipment and storage. Compared with earlier solutions, this proposal was more compact and its end pavilions were less susceptible to being read as separate entities.[101] The building had lost its tri-party symbolic meaning. Most people, it was thought, would come by streetcar, and any automobiles could be left on the street or in front of houses with little or no difficulty.

The drawings for this proposal evidence a historical rather than a technical classification for the art collection, and there were no special rooms for precious

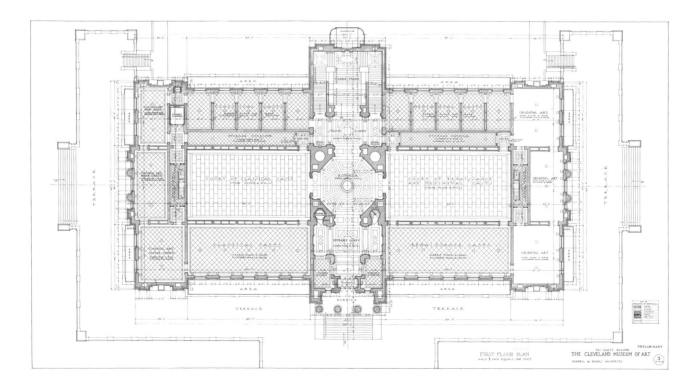

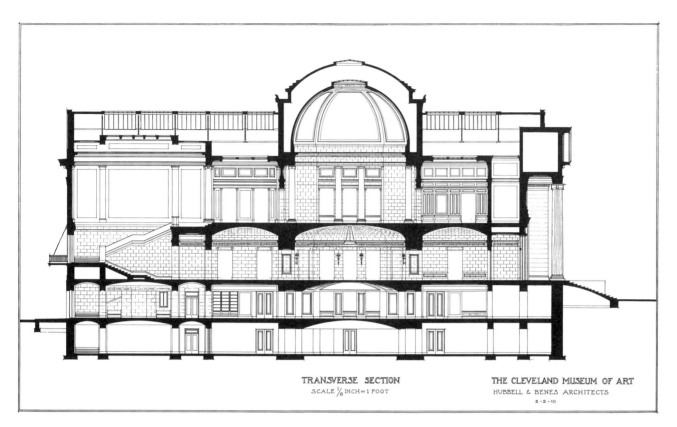

TRANSVERSE SECTION
SCALE ⅛ INCH = 1 FOOT

THE CLEVELAND MUSEUM OF ART
HUBBELL & BENES ARCHITECTS
2-2-10

Figure 18. Plan, section, and elevation drawings, from a set of working drawings made in 1910, for the building as initially approved in 1909, Hubbell and Benes, Cleveland Museum of Art.

This palatial architectural scheme was abandoned by 1911 due to its high cost.

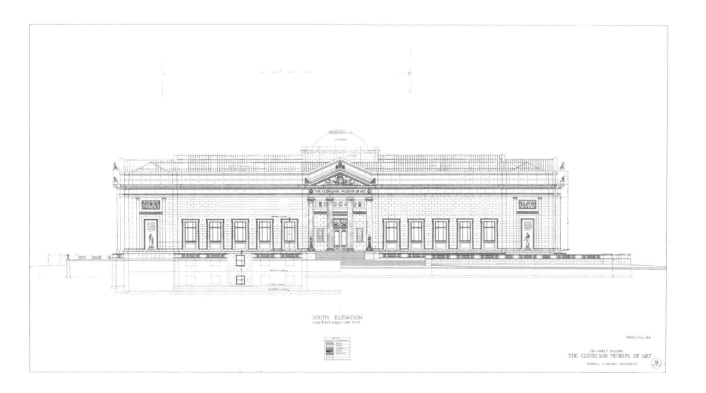

SOUTH ELEVATION
SCALE ⅛ INCH EQUALS ONE FOOT

THE CLEVELAND MUSEUM OF ART
HUBBELL & BENES ARCHITECTS

objects. All were to be considered important. However, the major spaces were designed primarily for a collection of plaster casts, probably under the stress of necessity, since there was virtually no budget for acquisitions. (By contrast, Boston during the period 1895-1904 had spent $1,324,683.62 on purchases alone.)[102] Edward Robinson, who had been consulted earlier on the plans, had written two books on the cast collections at Boston and New York, believing in their validity as educational tools. Casts could offer a completeness and unity not found in a museum of originals. Furthermore, because originals were beyond their means, many thought that cast collections must be the main dependence of American museums. Others, however, called them the "Pianola of the arts," believing, like Aristotle, that the direct aim of art is the pleasure derived from the contemplation of the perfect. The disruptions of World War I, however, were to prevent the Museum from acquiring more than a few casts, while the ensuing social, economic, and political shifts were to release treasures previously thought to be permanently housed abroad, providing American museums with opportunities for collecting great works of art.

1. The resolution to appoint the committee was made by William Sanders, seconded by Henry Ranney; Perkins instructed the committee to elect its own officials. Minutes of the John Huntington Art and Polytechnic Trust, June 7, 1905, vol. 1, CMA Archives.

2. Minutes of the Building Committee, Corporate, CMA Archives; *Cleveland Plain Dealer*, June 9, 1905. They personally met with John J. Albright. See "Report of the Building Committee, July 13, 1910," Building Committee Records, Corporate, CMA Archives.

3. Minutes of the Cleveland Chapter of the American Institute of Architects, June 10, 1905, MS. 4120, folder 141-2, Western Reserve Historical Society; Minutes of the Directory, Cleveland Chamber of Commerce, June 13, 1905, MS. 3471, Western Reserve Historical Society; *Cleveland Plain Dealer*, June 18, 1905.

4. F. S. Barnum, President, Cleveland Chapter, American Institute of Architects, quoted in *Cleveland Plain Dealer*, June 11, 1905.

5. Memorandum to Building Committee, October 6, 1902, Building Committee folder, 1902-1909, Archival Collection, Museum of Fine Arts, Boston.

6. *Cleveland Plain Dealer*, June 25, 1905.

7. Meeting of November 1, 1905.

8. Samuel Warren to Wheelwright, November 23, 1905. Six members of the Boston building committee voted in favor, one objected to loaning Wheelwright the material. Warren hoped that Cleveland would reward Wheelwright with the commission. See Wheelwright to Warren, November 24, 1905, thanking him for permission to make use of the "data on foreign museums." BAG.AC1, folder 92, Edmund Wheelwright, 1905-1910, Archival Collection, Museum of Fine Arts, Boston.

9. Wheelwright to Warren, November 29, 1905, in which he listed the items he borrowed for his presentation in Cleveland. Wheelwright exhibited the following plans: Industrial Museum—Berlin, Court of the Belvedere, Hertford House, New Museum at Hanover, Museum at Cassel, Art Museum—Vienna, Braccio Nuovo, National Bavarian Museum, Naples, Dresden, Amsterdam, Brera, Kaiser Frederick, Zurich, and Darmstadt. Section drawings included Hanover, loft over picture galleries; Darmstadt, picture gallery; and various other European galleries. BAG.AC1, folder 92, Edmund Wheelwright, 1905-1910, Archival Collection, Museum of Fine Arts, Boston.

10. Minutes of the Building Committee, June 4, 1906, CMA Archives.

11. The rationale was later summarized. Hermon Kelley to John D. Rockefeller, September 1910, Kelley-Huntington Trusts file, Corporate, CMA Archives; for a biography of Wheelwright, see "Edmund March Wheelwright, '76," *The Harvard Graduates' Magazine* 21 (December 1912): 240-242.

12. CMA Ingalls Library.

13. Secretary of the Building Committee to its members, January 5, 1906. The minutes of the meeting are not preserved. Corporate, CMA Archives.

14. Minutes of the Committee on Art Gallery [the original members of the committee were H. H. Johnson, J. D. Cox, M. S. Greenough, D. Z. Norton, and Charles L. Pack; by April 1906 Andrew Squire had replaced D. Z. Norton], January 25, March 30, 1906; Minutes of the Directory, April 19, 1906, Cleveland Chamber of Commerce, MS. 3471, Western Reserve Historical Society.

15. Cleveland, *City Council Proceedings*, file 6629, December 17, 1906, Petition from H. A. Kelley.

16. Cleveland, *City Council Proceedings*, file 6629, December 17, 1906, Petition from H. A. Kelley, file 4506, May 21, 1906.

17. For Holden's response of June 9, 1906, see Cleveland, *City Council Proceedings*, file 4824, June 11, 1906. It was published in part, see "A New Art Museum," *Ohio Architect and Builder* 7, 6 (June 1906): 41-42.

18. Cleveland, *City Council Proceedings*, file 4862, June 11, 1906.

19. Cleveland, *City Council Proceedings*, City Solicitor to Council, file 5078, mentioning Holden communication of June 9, 1906, June 25, 1906; *Cleveland Plain Dealer*, June 26, 1906.

20. Homer H. Johnson, "Cleveland's Opportunity in Art," *The Ohio Architect and Builder* 7, 6 (June 1906): 13-19.

21. Cleveland Chamber of Commerce, October 16, 1906, MS. 3471, Western Reserve Historical Society. Kenyon Cox's address was printed. The copy in the CMA Ingalls Library was presented by Hermon Kelley. Cox's idea for a museum of photographs was not new. See William Martin Conway, *The Domain of Art* (New York: E. P. Dutton, 1902), and "A Museum of Photographs," *Architectural Record* 12 (August 1902): 348-350.

22. Minutes of the Art Gallery Committee, May 8, 1907, Cleveland Chamber of Commerce, MS. 3471, Western Reserve Historical Society.

23. Minutes of the Building Committee, June 29, 1906, Corporate, CMA Archives.

24. Dyer may have shown his proposal in the Cleveland Architectural Club's exhibition of 1909, for he entered drawings labeled "An Art Museum." See *Catalogue of the Architectural Exhibition of the Cleveland Architectural Club* (Cleveland: The Caxton Co., 1909).

25. "The Work of Mr. J. Milton Dyer," *Architectural Record* 20, 5 (November 1906): 384-403.

26. The prototype for this was surely the new entrance hall of the Metropolitan Museum of Art, which had opened in 1902. Designed by Richard Morris Hunt, it was described as "the best classic building in this country." See Morrison H. Heckscher, "Hunt and the Metropolitan Museum of Art," in Susan R. Stein, ed., *The Architecture of Richard Morris Hunt* (Chicago: University of Chicago Press, 1986), 173.

27. Undated single sheet, citing comparative data on various museums from around the world. CMA Archives.

28. Minutes of the Building Committee, July 3 and 19, 1906, Corporate, CMA Archives.

29. Notes of interview with Edmund Wheelwright, December 12, 1905; notes of interview with Sturgis, December 13, 1905, Building Committee folder, 1902-1909, Archival Collection, Museum of Fine Arts, Boston.

30. Warren to Wheelwright, January 26, 1906; Wheelwright to Hunnewell, March 11, 1907, BAG.AC1, folder 92, Edmund Wheelwright, 1905-1910, Archival Collection, Museum of Fine Arts, Boston.

31. Secretary of the Building Committee to its members, July 25, 1906, Business Office, CMA Archives.

32. "Architects for Museum," *The Ohio Architect and Builder* 8, 4 (October 1906): 41.

33. Newspaper clipping, November 3, 1927, Vertical File, Cleveland Architects, A to B, Fine Arts Department, Cleveland Public Library.

34. The other members of the committee were Ranney, chairman *ex officio*; Thomas H. White; Julius E. French; and Harry A. Garfield. Meeting of the Board of Trustees, December 1895, Record Book no. 2, Administration, 1/M/1, Box 3. Apparently, they considered a design by C. F. Schweinfurth for the building (Schweinfurth to C. W. Bingham, September 6, 1895, Correspondence, 2/AC, Box 4). When the building was completed, Wade was thanked "for his careful and constant attention in looking after the new building ...," Annual Meeting of the Western Reserve Historical Society, May 3, 1898, Minutes of Meetings, Administration, 1/M/1, Box 3, Archives, Western Reserve Historical Society.

35. Wixom, *Cleveland Institute of Art*, 21.

36. See Joanne M. Lewis, *To Market To Market: An Old-Fashioned Family Story: The West Side Market* (Cleveland Heights, OH: Elandon Books, 1981).

37. B. S. Hubbell, typescript of a talk, Cleveland Chamber of Commerce, March 23, 1909, MS. 3471, Western Reserve Historical Society.

38. Benjamin S. Hubbell, "Building an Art Museum," *The Cornell Architect* 2, 1 (February 1916): 3.

39. Benjamin S. Hubbell, "The Cleveland Museum of Art," *Journal of the Cleveland Engineering Society* 6 (November 1913): 169-170.

40. He made this statement with reference to Boston. See Wheelwright to Samuel Warren, December 23, 1904, BAG.AC1, folder 91, Wheelwright Correspondence, Archival Collection, Museum of Fine Arts, Boston.

41. Edmund M. Wheelwright, "Art Galleries, Their Lighting, Heating and Ventilation, to Liberty E. Holden, Chairman, Building Committee, Cleveland Museum of Art," typescript, n.d., Records of the Building Committee, Corporate, CMA Archives. Although undated, this report was written at the beginning of the design process, because it does not critique any specific design, but only makes suggestions as to what should be done.

42. C. W. Fuller to Hubbell and Benes, May 16, 1907. Earlier Fuller wrote to Ranney as President of the Cleveland Museum of Art [now the Horace Kelley Art Foundation] requesting information on whether it would immediately proceed with construction and, if so, to fix the appropriate amount to be expended in the erection of the building to guide the architects, January 12, 1907. The budget was probably determined at a meeting of the Building Committee for May 16, 1907, the minutes for which are not preserved. On May 14, 1907, Fuller had sent members an announcement that it would take place. Apparently, Wheelwright attended this meeting. Corporate, CMA Archives.

43. Hermon Kelley, Secretary and Treasurer, Cleveland Museum of Art [now the Horace Kelley Art Foundation], to John D. Rockefeller, September 1910, Kelley-Huntington Trusts file, Corporate, CMA Archives.

44. Wheelwright had considerable experience in criticizing Sturgis's plan for the Boston Museum of Fine Arts. See, for example, Wheelwright to Samuel Warren, March 1, 1905: "setback on Huntington Avenue too narrow for good architectural effect or for freedom of lighting." BAG.AC1, folder 91, Wheelwright Correspondence, Archival Collection, Museum of Fine Arts, Boston.

45. *Cleveland Plain Dealer*, January 28, 1910.

46. Wheelwright to Samuel Warren, 1904, BAG.AC1, folder 91, Wheelwright Correspondence, Archival Collection, Museum of Fine Arts, Boston.

47. See, for example, John Cotton Dana, *The New Relations of Museums and Industries* (Newark: The Newark Museum Association, 1919), 13.

48. For a biography of Robinson, see Winifred E. Howe, *A History of the Metropolitan Museum of Art* (New York, 1913), 1: 293-294.

49. Hubbell, "Building an Art Museum," 3.

50. *Cleveland Plain Dealer*, November 17, 1907; Hubbell and Benes, Plat Drawing, no. 5-f, 12-30-07. This drawing cannot be located but is later mentioned. See Minutes of the Cleveland Museum of Art [now the Horace Kelley Art Foundation], June 6, 1908, Record Book no. 2.

51. The negotiations with Wade continued on well into 1908. See, for example, Holden to Johnson, July 23, 1908, Tom L. Johnson Papers, MS. 3651, Western Reserve Historical Society.

52. *Cleveland Plain Dealer*, January 29, 1910.

53. Minutes of the Cleveland Museum of Art [now the Horace Kelley Art Foundation], June 6, 1908, Record Book no. 2; Minutes of the John Huntington Art and Polytechnic Trust, June 12, 1908, vol. 1, CMA Archives. At these meetings both organizations approved the contract with Hubbell and Benes and with Wheelwright. The architects agreed to wait for 25 percent of their fees until the Hurlbut Trustees were in a position to pay.

54. B. S. Hubbell, typescript of talk, Cleveland Chamber of Commerce, March 23, 1909, MS. 3471, Western Reserve Historical Society.

55. Gries to Johnson, November 20, 1907, Tom L. Johnson Papers, MS. 3651, Western Reserve Historical Society. Gries did not feel the Adelbert Road plan was the best and suggested this alternative.

56. *Cleveland Plain Dealer*, January 29, 1910.

57. Ibid.

58. Minutes of the Building Committee, December 2, 1908, Corporate, CMA Archives. Wheelwright was at this meeting; Wheelwright and the Cleveland Chapter of the American Institute of Architects were entertained on December 3, 1908, at the Colonial Club. For the committee's reaction to the plan, see *Cleveland Leader*, December 4, 1908.

59. *Cleveland Plain Dealer*, December 19, 1908.

60. Ibid., January 17, 1909.

61. Meeting of the Trustees of the Cleveland Museum of Art [now the Horace Kelley Art Foundation] with Hubbell and Benes, December 2, 1908, Record Book no. 2, CMA Archives. The minutes describe the site plan as "plat-5d dated 8-13-08," and the plan as "no. 13-b dated 12-23-07." They also inspected a plaster model.

62. *Cleveland Plain Dealer*, December 19, 1908.

63. Margaret J. H. Smith et al. to The Trustees of the John Huntington Museum of Art, December 31, 1908, John Huntington Estate file, Harold T. Clark Papers, CMA Archives.

64. "Cost of Plan 'A,' the City Plan as Calculated by F. A. Pease Engineering Company," undated: $66,764. Cost of plan "B," as developed by Hubbell and Benes, was given in the same estimate as $50,550. 1916 Building file, Corporate, CMA Archives.

65. Wheelwright to Tom L. Johnson and C. W. Fuller, 1909, draft, Interchange of Land, Corporate, CMA Archives.

66. Under the date May 17, 1909, Minutes of the Building Committee, May 19, 1909, Corporate, CMA Archives.

67. Wheelwright to Fuller, May 31, 1909, 1916 Building file, Corporate, CMA Archives. Johnson was adamant that it be placed in the deed; Baker would have accepted another vehicle. *Cleveland Plain Dealer*, March 29, 1910; Baker wrote up a suggested form of covenant for free Days (Baker to T. L. Johnson, May 20, 1909). Wheelwright did not participate in the negotiations over free days (Baker to Holden, May 20, 1909). Baker insisted that all plantings, contours, etc., must be done by the Park Department rather than under private contract (Baker to Wheelwright, May 18, 1909). Newton D.

Baker Papers, MS. 3867, cont. 10, folder 3, nos. 287, 286, 279, Western Reserve Historical Society.

68. The date of the meeting was August 18, 1909. See "Report of the Sub-Committee for exchange of lands to the Building Committee." The exact free day requirement is articulated in Baker to Fuller, August 18, 1909, 1916 Building file, Corporate, CMA Archives.

69. *Cleveland Plain Dealer*, September 2, 1909.

70. Baker to Fuller, September 9, 1909, 1916 Building file, Corporate, CMA Archives. Baker cites Fuller's letter of September 8 and a copy of a letter from Holden to Johnson.

71. Minutes of the Building Committee, December 9, 1909, Corporate, CMA Archives.

72. Minutes of the Cleveland Museum of Art [now the Horace Kelley Art Foundation], Record Book no. 2, April 5, 1911.

73. Hubbell and Benes to C. W. Fuller, July 12, 1910, Records of the Building Committee, Corporate, CMA Archives.

74. Formal Report of the Building Committee, July 13, 1910, Corporate, CMA Archives.

75. Memorandum, November 9, 1936, concerning talk with Henry W. Kent, July 5, 1936. Henry W. Kent file, Harold T. Clark Papers, CMA Archives. Kent recalled that Baker was helpful in connection with the land exchange.

76. *Cleveland Plain Dealer*, January 27 and 28, 1910.

77. Ibid., January 29, 1910.

78. Ibid., February 3, 1912. This was before a meeting of club women at the Cleveland School of Art.

79. Ibid., February 23, 1910.

80. Cleveland, *City Council Proceedings*, file 17097, March 3, 1910.

81. Minutes of the Building Committee, March 4, 1910, Corporate, CMA Archives.

82. *Cleveland Press*, March 12, 1910; "Art Museum Coming," *The Ohio Architect and Builder* 15, 3 (March 1910): 51.

83. Cleveland, *City Council Proceedings*, Ordinance no. 17285, March 21, 1910.

84. *Cleveland Plain Dealer*, March 22, 1910.

85. Cleveland, *City Council Proceedings*, Ordinance no. 17285A; "Statement of the Art Museum Situation re exchange of lands in Wade Park with the City, May 20, 1910," Cleveland City Council file, Corporate, CMA Archives.

86. L. E. Holden and H. A. Kelley to Baehr, March 25, 1910, printed in *Cleveland Plain Dealer*, March 26, 1910.

87. Minutes of the John Huntington Art and Polytechnic Trust, January 29, 1910, CMA Archives.

88. This question was raised later by Joseph Hidy of Hidy, Klein and Harris, who filed a lawsuit against the Trustees in 1911 for the state Attorney General. See *Cleveland Plain Dealer*, July 12, 1911.

89. *Cleveland Plain Dealer*, March 26, 1910.

90. From Hurlbut's will, probated April 21, 1884; the income from the estate between April 21, 1884, to January 1, 1888, totaled $56,381.99. Cuyahoga County Probate Court, Docket L, no. 1466; and Bequests, Wills, Estates, and Funds, Hinman Hurlbut file, Director Turner, CMA Archives.

91. Minutes of the Cleveland Museum of Art [now the Horace Kelley Art Foundation], Record Book no. 2, April 5, 1911.

92. Minutes of the John Huntington Art and Polytechnic Trust, January 29, 1910, CMA Archives.

93. *Cleveland Plain Dealer*, March 26, 1910.

94. Ibid., March 29 and April 16, 1910.

95. Ibid., April 16, 1910.

96. Ibid., June 18, 1910.

97. Ibid., June 18 and 20, 1910.

98. Ibid., July 9, 1910.

99. On roll call, four of the Democrats voted adversely. Two wanted the gallery to be located downtown on the Mall. *Cleveland Plain Dealer*, July 12, 1910.

100. "Get the Art Museum," *The Ohio Architect and Builder* 16, 1 (July 1910): 11.

101. Linen Drawings dated March 14, 1910, Hubbell and Benes, CMA Archives.

102. Walter Muir Whitehill, *Museum of Fine Arts Boston, A Centennial History*, 2 vols. (Cambridge, MA: Harvard University Press, 1970), 1: 197.

THE POWER OF
CONSENSUS

Once the ideal site had been secured and working drawings were in hand, unforeseen financial difficulties held up construction. Not only did the Trustees face the $250,000-$300,000 shortfall from the loss of the Hurlbut estate, but the bids for the building came in at $269,000 over the initial $1,000,000 budget.[1] The overage, the Building Committee complained, was due to "the unconquerable habit of architects not to include in the prescribed cost of a building such items as architect's fees (then already $40,000), landscaping and the like." They did acknowledge that the original building program, however, did not include a subbasement, which was now regarded as a necessity for completeness and convenience.

On July 7, 1910, for reasons of health, Liberty Holden resigned as chairman of the Building Committee. Since the Cleveland City Council had agreed to the exchange of land and the Museum organizers had approved the plans, this committee considered its work to be finished. In their final report the members recommended that a new committee be appointed with the power to let contracts, etc., and that a competent Director for the Museum be appointed at the earliest possible date, citing the repeated problem of the committee's inability to secure a quorum and the need for someone to devote his undivided attention to the enterprise. They regretted having undertaken the preparation of the plans without first having hired a Director, which they felt was essential for creating an interest in art, gaining community cooperation, and connecting the Museum with the art market which they felt was rapidly being exhausted by other museums. Later, William B. Sanders searched for potential candidates to fill this important position. Work on the building plans came to a virtual standstill in July 1910.[2]

In September the Trustees considered two alternatives: either find an additional $500,000 or reduce the budget to $750,000. While Charles W. Bingham thought each corporation should simply appropriate more funds, others warned that if they expended too much on the building, it would deplete the endowments and "seriously embarrass" the acquisition of works of art, the maintenance of the building, and possibly even the stability of the entire enterprise. J. H. Wade suggested that the architects sketch new plans for a smaller building—one that would satisfy their immediate needs—but H. R. Hatch proposed that rather than abandoning their plans they raise the shortfall. To this end, a delegation called on John D. Rockefeller at his East Cleveland residence (now Forest Hills Park, the house burned down in 1917) and sent a follow-up letter.[3] Although Rockefeller kept the plans overnight, their pleas went unheeded. In April 1911 the Trustees were still undecided as to what course of action they should take with regard to the building plans, whether to abandon or to continue with the ones approved in early 1910.[4]

Meanwhile, in January 1911, City Council asked the Trustees to report on their progress, and in March they asked the city's administration to do what it could to hasten construction.[5] Public pressure was beginning to build. By the end of May the state Attorney General, Timothy S. Hogan, was considering moves to call for a complete accounting to prove that enough money was on hand or an action *in mandamus* compelling the Trustees to start construction. In response, Hermon Kelley acknowledged that there was a problem. After calling the Attorney General's plan "tommyrot"—"The state authorities have no more to do with the museum than they have with my private estate"—he conceded that the "trustees of the art museum [the Kelley Trustees] are waiting for the Huntington estate trustees to come to some agreement with them."[6] As the Trustees got older and traveled more, they admittedly lost interest in the project. Some even professed complete ignorance of the Museum's affairs, and it was difficult to achieve a quorum for meetings. Five did not bother to attend a meeting for over a year. The force that kept the project going was Hermon A. Kelley, who was Secretary and Treasurer of the Kelley Foundation.[7]

The threatened legal action prodded the Trustees

into action, but did not stop the state from starting proceedings on July 11, 1911, in the Cuyahoga County Court of Common Pleas, to force an accounting and to begin construction; Hogan's attitude was that the Trustees were responsible to the public and were covered by a statute giving the state oversight of all trust funds.[8] The *Cleveland Leader* noted that Cleveland had doubled in population since the first promise of an art gallery for public use was given by the Kelley will and that many thousands of the men and women then living had since died. The newspaper called for a complete accounting in open court.[9] The Cleveland Chamber of Commerce thought differently, however, and sent a special committee to visit City Solicitor Newton D. Baker to head off the suits; their pleas were in vain.[10]

Simultaneous with the state's perusal of legal action, in June 1911, the Huntington and Kelley Trustees renewed negotiations—conference committees were appointed from each corporation to consult together on plans.[11] Both reaffirmed their intention to erect a joint building. The Kelley Foundation's Board attempted to strengthen the negotiations by electing Huntington Trustees Mariett Huntington (John Huntington's widow) and John Lowman as members. Nonetheless, in an attempt to gain greater independence, the Huntington Trustees tried to get actual title to the land, but Hermon Kelley held firm and would only grant a perpetual lease, an arrangement that had been agreed upon in 1905. The Huntington Trust, however, directed that its portion of the structure was to be called the "Huntington Museum." Both Boards agreed to put more money into the building to make up for the shortfall from the Hurlbut estate. But bids on the plans approved in March 1910 were still $269,000 over budget. Realizing they needed an expert on the job, they decided that they should secure the services of someone to supervise the work.[12]

To resolve these problems, in July 1911, a new joint Building Committee of five was constituted (Sanders, Bingham, and George H. Worthington, appointed by the Huntington Trust; and Wade and

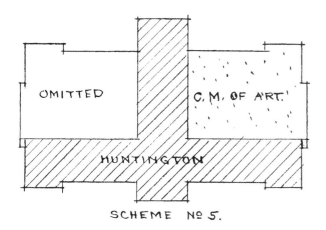

OMITTED   C. M. OF ART.

HUNTINGTON

SCHEME Nº 5.

Figure 19. One of at least five different proposals done during 1910 by Hubbell and Benes to reduce the cost of the proposed building. This one eliminates the entire northwest section of the building.

Kelley appointed by the Kelley Foundation). They were instructed to see if they could modify earlier plans for a building now to cost $900,000;[13] among other things, they spent the next few months seeking a museum expert who would both see the building through to completion and become the Museum's first Director. Of course, they did not advertise the job; they instead looked for potential candidates via the "old boy" system. In September 1911 J. H. Wade asked George Kunz of Tiffany and Company (who assisted J. P. Morgan in collecting art) to suggest a candidate. After Kunz spoke highly of Henry W. Kent, who was then Assistant Secretary at the Metropolitan Museum of Art, Wade discreetly found out whether he would be open to a proposition. Besides knowledge and experience—at that time no museum training or internship programs existed—Kent had a well-bred personality that the Trustees liked. At the end of November as one of three final candidates, he was offered the job at a salary of $5,000 per year—$1,400 more than Cornelia Sage was making as Director of The Albright Art Gallery. Although Kent declined the offer, he was retained as a consultant to the Building Committee, a job he began in January 1912. In September of the same year, based in part on Kent's recommendation (names were also obtained from the American Federation of the Arts), the Trustees offered the Museum's first directorship to Frederic Allen Whiting. Although he accepted in

January 1913,[14] Whiting came only after the plans for the building were substantially finished.

Concurrent with the search for a Director, the Building Committee considered the plans. Their first solution, in July 1911, responded to the urgency of the moment: to delete the entire northwest section of the building (Figure 19).[15] To this end the Huntington Trust agreed to erect the entire southern half and the great hall, while the Kelley Foundation would erect the northeastern quadrant.[16] Thus, the main facade facing south toward Euclid Avenue and the east facade on East Boulevard would be whole, creating an illusion of completeness to the casual passerby. The *Cleveland Plain Dealer* proclaimed that this solution had merit; not building the Hurlbut section would save a considerable number of fine trees.[17] The *Cleveland Leader* declared that the "incompleteness of the building ... [will] ... in itself ... [be] ... a constant appeal to civic pride and generosity."[18]

Hubbell and Benes were directed to prepare revised plans and to obtain bids for the "incomplete" building, which they did not do. French and Hubbard were instructed to prepare working drawings for the mechanical systems, and preparation of the site began (survey, soil tests, etc.). The architects were so unhappy about erecting an "incomplete" building that they prepared two alternative schemes for a complete, but one-story, museum on their own volition. Since the Trustees demanded an imposing edifice—a few

months earlier, Bingham stated that he did not believe that a "suitable building representing the Huntington trust" could be built for under $1 million[19]
—Hubbell shrewdly argued that a one-story structure
was actually more in scale with the surrounding park
and residential environment. He even devised a clever
stratagem to drive home the point that such a building would be suitably impressive. Over the weekend
of October 23, 1911, he had 60-foot-tall telephone
poles erected along the front and corners of the proposed building, across which was suspended white
bunting at the proposed cornice height of the one-
story building (Figure 20). The one-story scheme was
planned with unusually high ceilings and a sufficiently
heavy coping to prevent the building from looking
flat or "squatty."[20] (Two years earlier, to test his
ideas, Hubbell had simply drawn their proposal on
actual photographs taken of the site. See Figure 21.)

When the Building Committee came to the architects' offices on October 30, the architects not only
presented plans for an "incomplete" building but
plans for a "complete" one as well.[21] Not getting very
far with the full committee, Hubbell, in a calculated
move, invited Mrs. Huntington, who was also a
Huntington Trustee, to view his latest proposal (Figure 22),[22] which included an important selling point:
although physically smaller, the actual exhibition
space would be greater and all on one floor, a distinct
advantage to visitors. In addition more room would
be allocated for education. Deleting the monumental
interior stair hall, which decorum and tradition dictated for a two-story building, would save space.
Furthermore, the architects had a conference with
Mayor-elect Newton D. Baker, who then pledged
his support for placing a power plant in Wade Park
immediately west of the site,[23] eliminating the need
for a subbasement boiler room and consequently for
a smoke stack, which would have ruined the roof line
of the building. It would also be possible to build
an extension on the north side for more exhibition

Figure 20. On October 23, 1911, the architects had white bunting strung between telephone poles erected on the museum site to illustrate how their proposal for a single-story building would relate to the surrounding neighborhood.

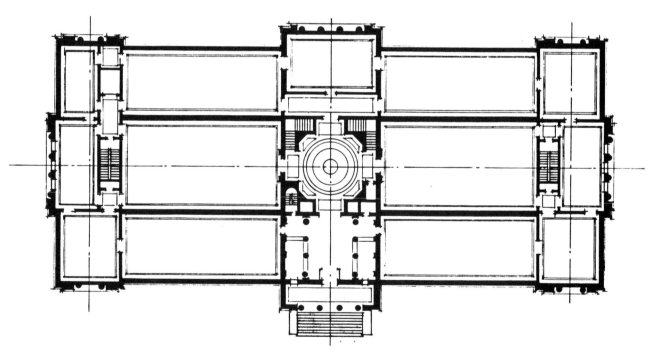

Figure 22. The idea for a museum planned around a central rotunda goes back at least to the late eighteenth century and was by the beginning of the twentieth century a common feature in public buildings. Proposal for a "complete" one story building, November 16, 1911, Hubbell and Benes, Cleveland Museum of Art.

space and education space at later date should the need arise.

Mrs. Huntington immediately favored the one-story version—as did Sanders. Caught off guard, Bingham, the chairman of the committee, expressed his displeasure that the committee's mandate to secure bids on the "incomplete" proposal was being ignored by the architects. For all intents and purposes the decision was already made, but the committee hesitated and continued to study its options, thus driving the architects to guarantee that their extra charges for a new one-story design would have a $10,000 cap (they were, of course, to be paid an additional amount for supervising construction). Consequently, as a result of the architects' tenacity and political acumen—in combination with the committee's conservative character—the plan for a complete building was ratified.[24] One other factor played a role: while everyone recognized that the cost of this solution would exceed the projected budget, both corpo-

rations had assets that were rapidly escalating in value. The John Huntington Art and Polytechnic Trust held a large block of Standard Oil stock and the Kelley Foundation owned downtown property adjacent to the announced locations for a new, high level bridge—the Detroit-Superior, opened in 1917—and even better, for a new suburban railway terminal to be built by the Van Sweringen interests (now Tower City).[25] This scheme constituted the embryo for the museum that was actually constructed.

Although the design is two stories in height, the ground service floor is level with the natural grade on the north, while the first exhibition floor is raised 14-1/2 feet above this level by means of terraces and staircases on the south (Figure 23). Therefore, the south, main facade, when viewed across the Wade Park lagoon from Euclid Avenue, gives the appearance of being a one-story structure with an uncomplicated profile. From the south the exhibition floor is directly approached by a series of exterior monumen-

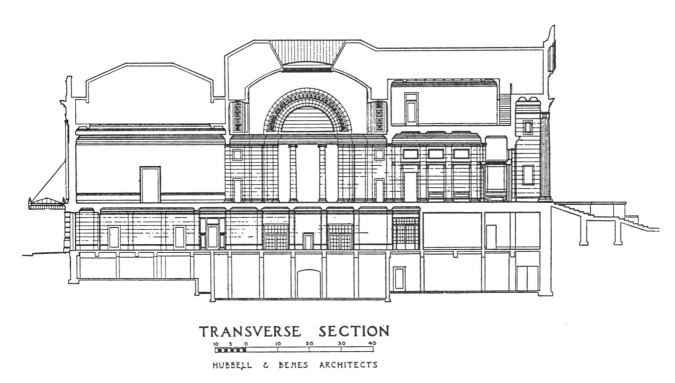

Figure 23. The design is really two stories in height, the ground floor level with the grade on the north, while the first floor is raised 14-½ feet above ground level by means of terraces and steps on the south. Transverse section, as built, 1916, Hubbell and Benes, Cleveland Museum of Art.

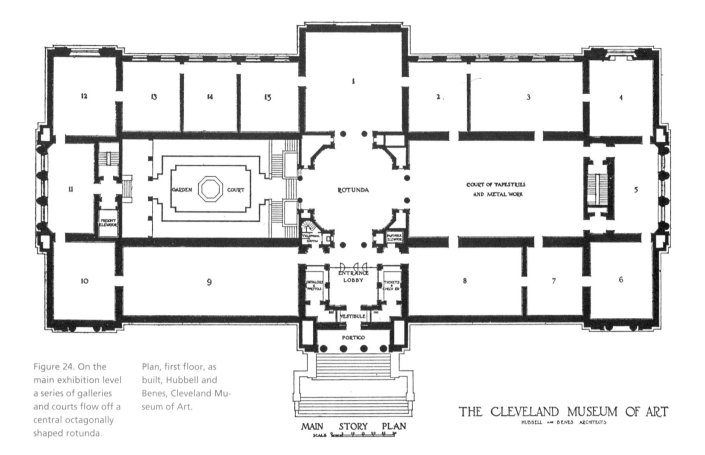

Figure 24. On the main exhibition level a series of galleries and courts flow off a central octagonally shaped rotunda.

Plan, first floor, as built, Hubbell and Benes, Cleveland Museum of Art.

tal stairs and terraces, which increases the visual pretense and monumentality of the structure. Thus, the total composition and architectural detailing avoided any appearance of parsimony or meanness. This solution was also economical; an exterior approach to the exhibition floor saved the cost of constructing a monumental stair hall on the interior.

Like the exterior, the interior arrangement was decidedly simple, convenient, and symmetrical (Figure 24). The main entrance opens through a portico on the southern facade that leads past a public service area, containing a counter where coats could be checked and tickets and catalogues purchased, into the main exhibition area. A large, octagonally shaped rotunda forms the core of the building—the place where people gather, disperse, and reunite. Off the rotunda, to the east and west are two courts, each 46 by 85 feet and slightly over 34 feet high: a court of casts (now the Armor Court) and a garden court. Surrounding these great spaces, which aid in the circulation of visitors, are a series of exhibition galleries and

rooms of different dimensions, connecting with one another and with the central courts, permitting the Museum visitor to explore numerous alternative pathways through the galleries. This symmetry of plan not only allows visitors to comprehend where they are in the building easily, but reflects early twentieth-century architectural theory. For Otto Wagner—an architectural theorist that Hubbell surely read—"there was something decided, completed, well-weighed, incapable of extension, indeed self-conscious in a symmetrical design, which is required by earnestness and dignity, the constant attendants of architecture."[26] All the galleries, except those on the south, had provision for overhead light as well as side light, one or the other to be excluded according to the needs of the objects exhibited.

The lower, ground floor was planned to include the executive offices, conference room, receiving and shipping rooms, repair rooms, and so forth (Figures 25–28). Provisions were made for the staff and the care of the building, as well as storerooms, educa-

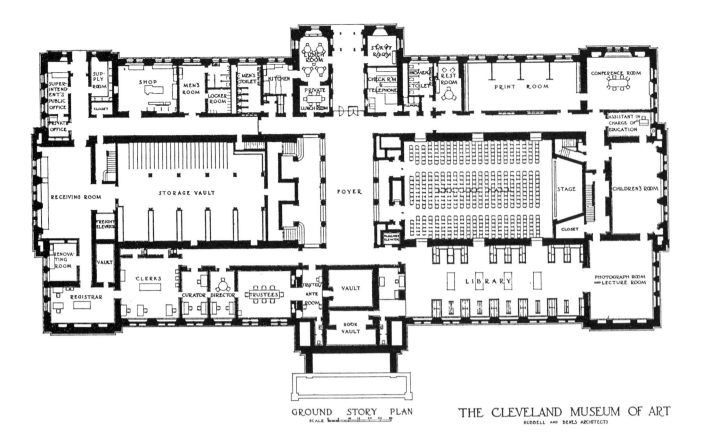

GROUND STORY PLAN
SCALE

THE CLEVELAND MUSEUM OF ART
HUBBELL AND BENES ARCHITECTS

Figure 25. The ground floor housed the support services necessary for the Museum's operation as well as classrooms, library, and a lecture hall.

Plan, ground floor, as built, Hubbell and Benes, Cleveland Museum of Art.

tional workrooms, classrooms, a library for 10,000 books, and a lecture hall for 450 persons, which was approached by stairs from the main rotunda. Public service rooms—such as toilets and extra checkrooms —were included. A lunch room, located near the carriage entrance on the north facade, completed the amenities offered to the Museum patron. By placing a door directly onto the entrance lobby before the turnstiles to the Museum, park users could dine without paying the entrance fee and, simultaneously, the increase in business would help to create the critical mass necessary for a more economical operation.

In the first architectural scheme of late 1911, the primary staircases connecting the two major levels were to be located in the leftover spaces between the octagonal rotunda and the rectangular galleries (Figure 22). These locations were soon rejected in favor of a double, more monumental and gracious staircase that gives access from the rotunda through the garden court to the lower level (Figure 29) and thereby allows natural light to penetrate down into the lobby area in front of the lecture hall. The basic configuration of the rotunda, however, was retained—a service stair for employees was located in one corner, and a passenger elevator for patrons in another.

Level with Euclid Avenue, the Museum building is 24 feet above the surface of the Wade Park lagoon (Figure 30). Informal paths were planned and eventu-

Figure 26. The original Trustees Room was located on the south side of the ground floor next to the Director's Office.

Figure 27. The Library was planned to have enough space for 10,000 books and to accommodate the public as well as staff.

Figure 28. Located adjacent to the north entrance, the Lunch Room could also serve visitors from Wade Park.

Figure 29. The ground floor foyer opposite the Lecture-Hall was connected by means of a monumental stairway through the Garden Court to the main exhibition level. Natural light from above reinforced the visual and symbolic linkage between the educational and exhibition functions of the Museum.

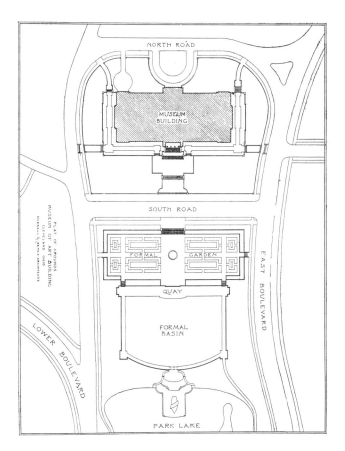

Figure 30. Proposed site plan, 1916, Hubbell and Benes, Cleveland Museum of Art.

ally built to surround the lagoon, along which pedestrians could approach the Museum after arriving at University Circle by streetcar. A fountain at the north end of the lake was conceived—though never executed—to be the poetic expression of the thought that Science, Literature, and Art are made possible by Commerce and Industry (Figure 31). Designed by Herman Matzen, it represented the Ship of Culture under swelling sail. Before the mast Matzen envisioned a group of three figures representing Science, Literature, and Art. At the helm stood Culture, while surmounting the prow was a rising figure of Pegasus. Beyond the ship was planned a water cascade, with figures of Vulcan and Mercury, representing Industry and Commerce, on the sides. The fountain was to be constructed so that the flowing sail and the artificial movement to the water would give apparent motion to the ship.

A proposed shallow pool, north of the cascade, was to provide a place where children could sail their boats and to reflect the outlines of the building, thus adding to the decorative effect during the day and in the evening when the lamps were lit. This was to be followed by a formal Italian garden with a fountain, seats, and statuary. Hubbell thought it should be a Garden of Fame where busts and tablets of distinguished Cleveland men could be properly placed. It was to be a quiet place for rest and reflection. From the architectural standpoint, however, it was also to provide a formal approach, which Hubbell deemed essential, to the "refined lines" of classical architecture. Visually, it would serve as a transitional area, smoothly integrating the organic, romantic, shapes of the lake and its surroundings with the geometric, formal shape of the Museum building. The building was to be separated from the garden by a flight of steps and a roadway which was planned and built (later removed) for the convenience of those being dropped off by automobile: vehicles could loop around from Euclid Avenue and return without making a U-turn.

The final form of the building was derived from a simple, severe Greek temple (Figure 32). In the early

Figure 31. The architects hoped to entice the city or other benefactor to pay for extensive landscaping and development of the site adjacent to the Museum. Plaster model of the proposed building and site, 1912, Hubbell and Benes, Cleveland Museum of Art.

twentieth century, it was understood that a museum was a natural extension of the classical temple. The temple was the home of a god, the deity represented by a statue occupying a place of honor inside. Out of devotion, the followers of the deity lavished on the temple the highest artistic expression. Over time, the temple became the treasure house in which was deposited society's most precious objects. It was said in 1905 with reference to the Albright Art Gallery, which Cleveland's Trustees regarded as their model, that the temple of one age became the museum of another, and its form was, therefore, appropriate for an art gallery.[27] Simultaneously, one of the essential at-

tributes of Greek architecture was considered to be clarity—the distinct expression of purpose—which was believed to be the inseparable companion of taste.[28] Furthermore, they felt that Greek art possessed not mere sensuousness, but beauty tempered by intellectual and moral qualities that made it noble and elevating to those who became imbued with its spirit. It was thought that an art gallery should be so impressive in its dignity that people would approach it with a certain feeling of reverence, a feeling calculated to intensify the responsibility and duty of citizens having a personal participatory interest in the structure and its contents.[29]

Figure 32. Rendering of proposed south facade, 1912, Hubbell and Benes, Cleveland Museum of Art.

Incord About Severance

Accordingly, the central portico consists of four majestic monolithic fluted Ionic columns surmounted by a pediment (Figures 33-35). The Ionic order was seen as exemplifying the spirit of feminine grace, lightness, dignity, and refinement, as distinguished from the massiveness and severity of the Doric and the too luxurious Corinthian. Again, the Trustees may have asked Hubbell to use the Ionic style because of the Albright Art Gallery's example; its appearance in his earlier proposals shows that it was not a last-minute or arbitrary decision. The austere roof line is relieved only by ornaments (*acroteria*) placed at the apex and ends of the portico's pediment (Figure 36).

Tablets on either side of the bronze front doors pay tribute to the founders. On each side of the portico plain walls extend to the flanking end-pavilions, and are adorned with two Ionic columns between which Hubbell proposed placing marble sculptures: the one on the east representing Michelangelo, the great advocate of form; the one on the west representing Titian, the exponent of color. As Paolo Pino explained it in the sixteenth century: "If Titian and Michelangelo were a single body, or if to Michelangelo's drawing were added the coloring of Titian, the artist might be called the god of painting."[30] In 1915—perhaps for economic reasons, since by then the building was way over budget—it was decided to omit these sculpted figures. But the originally intended inscription, *Architecture, Painting, Sculpture*, over the main entrance was replaced by decorative panels, because it served no real purpose and was not valuable architecturally.[31] Over time, therefore, the composition grew to be less literal and more abstract. Even the bronze and iron grills for the ground floor windows were to be of the "simplest possible design."[32]

Each end of the building is articulated with triple windows framed by a portico pattern. An equal number of columns on the ends as on the front (south) portico felicitously ties together the north and south facades—the two fronts—of the building (Figure 37). The north front was articulated with a series of windows and a *porte cochere* (Figure 38). Here, visitors had the opportunity of leaving their automobiles and entering without walking up monumental stairs. Once inside, they could then take either the passenger elevator or interior stairs up to the exhibition level; this increased accessibility for elderly and disabled patrons. From a purely functional point of view, this north entrance provided direct access to the classrooms, library, and lecture hall, thereby segregating internal pedestrian movement (children and non-gallery visitors would not have to pass through any part of the exhibition floor, preserving a sought-after reverent tone in the galleries). A service and business entrance was also located on the north side.

The total simplicity of the 300-foot-long main south facade—broad and plain, punctuated with a central portico—reflected not only an understanding of Greek architecture but was also in fact quite modern. The direct question "How should we build?" could not of course be answered, but Otto Wagner postulated:

our feeling must indeed say to us today that the antique horizontal line, the arrangement of surfaces in broad areas, the greatest simplicity, and an energetic prominence of construction and material will thoroughly dominate future developed and novel art forms; this is demanded by modern technical science and by the means at our command. It is self-evident that the beautiful expression, which architecture will give to the needs of our time, must harmonize with the views and with the appearance of modern mankind, and it must show the individuality of the architect.[33]

Thus, the exterior of the Museum was calculated to ennoble and to teach the greater truths to the citizens of Cleveland through classical form and, concurrently, to represent the modern age. The public got its first glimpse of the proposed design in November 1912, when two plaster models—one of the complete conception on a scale of 1/4 inch to a foot and a second of the entire south facade on a scale of 1-1/2 inches to the foot—were placed on display at The Cleveland School of Art.[34] The design represented by the models was that of the previous April, for their construction had kept workmen busy from that time

Inc

Figure 33. Plaster model of the proposed south (main) portico, 1912, Hubbell and Benes, Cleveland Museum of Art.

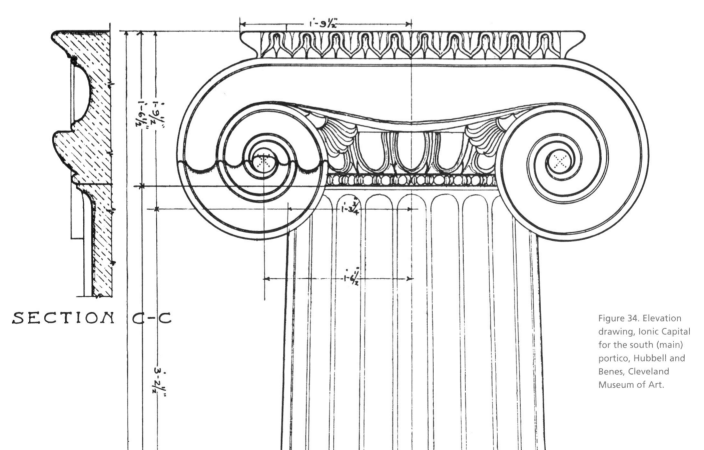

SECTION C-C

Figure 34. Elevation drawing, Ionic Capital for the south (main) portico, Hubbell and Benes, Cleveland Museum of Art.

Figure 35. Plaster model of south entrance detail. The architectural detailing was developed by means of such plaster models, which were then also used to guide the stone masons. Hubbell and Benes, Cleveland Museum of Art.

Figure 36. Detail drawing for the acroterium (the ornament placed at the apex of the pediment) on the south portico, Hubbell and Benes, Cleveland Museum of Art.

Figure 37. Terraces and balustrades effectively mask the lower ground floor level on the south, east, and west sides, making the building appear to have only one floor. The east and west sides of the building are articulated with four engaged columns.

Plaster model, 1912, Hubbell and Benes, Cleveland Museum of Art.

Figure 38. The Museum's north side had direct entrances to the offices, educational, and service support areas.

through the first week of November.[35] People viewing the models were enthusiastic about the proposed building, and a movement was launched to add the landscaping, forecourt, and sculptural additions that Hubbell had included in the site model.[36] He had wanted them shown to emphasize the necessity for developing such features.[37] At this time, a brochure was also published illustrating the plans.[38] These efforts to inform the public about the progress on the Museum were in response to the continuing suits started by the Ohio Attorney General's office to force a public accounting[39] and were part of a planned program to stimulate the community's interest in art before the Museum actually opened.

In 1912 Henry Kent not only acted as consultant to the Building Committee, but in September he also agreed to be its secretary with full power to represent the committee. By that time, they had so much confidence in him that they asked him to continue as consultant even if Whiting accepted the job as Director.[40] While the basic design remained that of Hubbell and

Benes, Kent made substantial changes during 1912 ensuring the efficient operation of the Museum and refining its architectural character.

First, knowing that many employees were involved when a work of art was acquired by a museum, Kent reviewed the physical layout with regard to the handling of objects during the acquisition process. He insisted that the operation be carried out efficiently, safely, and securely, since works of art are especially vulnerable in larger buildings. The Registrar's office, where objects are numbered, recorded, and tracked, was placed next to receiving (Figure 39), and he relocated the storage area from a subbasement to the ground floor[41] adjacent to receiving and increased its size. The Registrar's office connected directly to the clerks' and Director's offices and to the Board of Trustees Room, since it was the Board's responsibility to accept or purchase objects. Kent had presented the theoretical model on which this layout was based at a meeting of the American Association of Museums in May 1911.[42] Before that time, no American museum had adequate office space or storage; Kent's intervention made the Cleveland design unique. Kent also insisted on adequate provision for classrooms.

All the service functions were grouped together off a wide passageway with its own entrance, so that incoming objects could be unpacked and taken immediately to their intended destinations, whether that be storage, the Registrar's, or the preparation room for repair, etc., thereby increasing efficiency and strengthening security. The freight elevator was also located here, so that objects could be moved to the exhibition level or farther up to a photographer's studio. To protect objects during transport, all the corridors and door openings, even the height of the freight elevator, were suitably planned taking into account the objects' probable width, height, and the turning radii of carts. The storage room for paintings was equipped with a series of movable, sliding metal frames covered with metal netting for hanging the pictures (Figure 40). Suspended on a series of closely spaced tracks from the ceiling, any panel could be quickly pulled out. New at the time, this solution saved considerable floor space, besides making any painting immediately accessible.

With regard to the exhibition floor, Kent planned the division of rooms, taking into account the probable contents of each based on their lighting conditions. He also removed the beveled corners in all the galleries, except in the central gallery on the north. Furthermore, he removed the windows on each side of the main entrance,[43] making instead provision for toplighting the entrance hall. On the exterior a series of panels inscribed with the names of artists underneath the cornice on the south, east, and west facades of the building, which Hubbell had proposed, was omitted, thus making the building more severe.[44] With the general principle of the building assured, a struggle over its final details was to take place between Trustees, Building Committee, and architects.

In December 1912 Sanders drove the architects— he actually had a blow-up with them—to finish the drawings and the specifications, so bids could be let.

By February 1913 Hubbell had the specifications finished[45] and had everything ready for the heating and ventilating engineers, French and Hubbard, to continue with their work.

By the beginning of April the Building Committee had discussed at length the wisdom of employing a local firm, the Crowell and Sherman Company, as contractors.[46] The architects objected to this decision, not only because the contract would be awarded without competition, but because Crowell and Sherman did not have experience in building this type of structure.[47] Crowell and Sherman was a relatively small company; its capital stock was valued at $60,000 in 1913.[48] The President of the company, Benedict Crowell, however, was well established in Cleveland's business and social circles. He was on the Board of Directors of many Cleveland corporations. The Trustees had obviously decided to give the contract to someone they knew and, by doing so, supported a local enterprise. (Hubbell preferred a contractor from out of town.)

The agreement with the contractors, which underwent at least five or six drafts, was worked out between Hermon Kelley, the architects, representatives from Crowell, and a Mr. Stewart representing Crowell from Kelley's law firm, Hoyt, Dustin, Kelley, McKeehan, and Andrews. To avoid a conflict of interest, Kelley asked Sanders to scrutinize the draft contract, and he made suggestions such as requiring a personal bond of $250,000 from Crowell and a $50 per day penalty clause for delay. Since Sanders was powerful enough to assure that the agreement would be acceptable, he authorized the architects to instruct Crowell to begin construction on April 26, 1913, as well as to inform the newspapers about it.[49] The draft agreement was officially approved on May 5, 1913, by the Huntington Trust, but not without some changes in the delay clause.[50] The contractors guaranteed a base price with optional add-ons and agreed to work on an actual cost plus a commission basis. Crowell was to receive 10 percent on such trades as they would undertake themselves, plus 2 percent on all

Figure 39. The Receiving Room provided a large commodious area for unpacking and packing works of art and was conveniently located by the freight elevator and storage areas. The Cleveland Museum was one of the first to provide adequate facilities for these behind-the-scenes operations.

Figure 40. Innovative for its time, the painting storage system continues to function to the present day, although relocated in the 1958 wing. Depicted are Sherman E. Lee, Director of the Museum 1958-1983, with Emery May (Mrs. R. Henry) Norweb, granddaughter of Liberty Holden and President of the Museum Trustees 1962-1971.

subcontracts.[51] Since the design was far from complete, add-ons and design changes substantially raised the final cost to $1,308,531.66 (plus $129,577.95 for an auxiliary power plant),[52] well over the original 1907 budget of $1 million.

Meanwhile, in early 1912 Kelley and Sanders, representing the interests of the Kelley Foundation and Huntington Trust respectively, began to discuss the Museum's future operation. Sanders suggested that a common agency be arranged to assure strong management. Remember, since it was legally impossible to consolidate the corporations, the building only looked like it housed a single institution. In reality, it was to be internally divided by a party wall into two sections, one owned by the Kelley Foundation, the other by the Huntington Trust. Sanders wanted a new agency to manage both as one unit.[53] At first Kelley did not see the advantage of another corporation, but a few months later he proposed that the legal corporate name of the Kelley foundation—the Cleveland Museum of Art—be changed to the Horace Kelley Art Foundation, and that a new corporation be formed under the name *The Cleveland Museum of Art* to act as the operative company. At first this idea did not appeal to the Huntington Trustees. Because they did not closely identify with "The Cleveland Museum of Art," they demanded to have the Museum named after Huntington. Kelley, however, argued:

the principal object in using the name of The Cleveland Museum of Art … is the effect upon the public, particularly in the matter of donations … [We are] anxious to give the proposed museum a very broad foundation … full sympathy of the public … giving the people of Cleveland to understand that the institution is theirs.[54]

Discussion continued well into 1913, when there was some urgency to make a decision. The new Director, Frederic Allen Whiting, was about to arrive; Kelley thought it best to have an organization in place.[55] Sanders undertook to draft the articles of incorporation, which could be legally made under section 9972 of the Ohio code. Earlier, in fact, his law

firm had put through two charters along these general lines. Sanders suggested that the initial two-thirds of the Board members be appointed by the Huntington Trust, and one-third be appointed by the Kelley Foundation. After that, the Board would be self-perpetuating. Eventually, therefore, it would become a completely independent rather than a subsidiary body. In a mollifying tone, he hoped that both Kelley and Wade would be initial members.[56] On May 5, 1913, only after these basic principles were agreed on was the Building Committee re-appointed and constituted as a Committee on Organization. Thereafter, Sanders finished drafting the articles of incorporation with feedback from Kelley and Charles W. Bingham.[57]

The Articles of Incorporation bear the date June 25, 1913, and the new corporation held its first meeting in December 1913. By-laws were drafted, and the agreement between the Kelley Foundation and Huntington Trust (both of which continue to the present day) and the new corporation, largely written by Sanders, was signed on January 27, 1914. Since the trusts could not dispose of property, works purchased with their money remained their property; however, after considerable discussion with the aim of securing future donations—it was already clear that the Kelley and Huntington incomes would not be sufficient to operate the Museum—the new corporation could also own and purchase works in its own right. The agreement also compelled the Museum authorities to counsel freely with the two funding corporations as to all matters of general policy and dictated that no radical or extraordinary steps could be taken with reference to the conduct of the Museum without submission to and approval by them. Furthermore, an initial provision—rescinded in 1929—stipulated that if the operating agreement should be terminated, the building and any contents purchased with Kelley or Huntington funds would revert to them.[58] Thus, in 1913 The Cleveland Museum of Art came into being. Today, it is forgotten that the Museum was largely the creation of dexterous lawyers, who in the end saw to it that the Museum would not have the image of a private, "tribal" institution. Its essence was to be public, although it was—and remains—a private, not-for-profit institution.

Actual construction started before many of the architectural details could be agreed on or worked out, one of the most important being the exterior material of the superstructure (Figure 41). Kent felt not only that the decision for the exterior finish rested with the Huntington Trustees, but that the interior finish of the entrance hall, rotunda, and the court of casts also depended on that decision. The interior, he advised, should be different from the exterior for "variety and greater effectiveness."[59]

The question of exterior finish engendered heated debate and was under discussion from June through November 1913. The architects' recommendation, supported by Wade, was to have the lower level (the bottom 14-1/2 feet) faced with pink Milford Granite, the top to be of white marble. This combination had

been used for the Corcoran Gallery in Washington. Another suggestion called for the entire outside to be of Gray Canyon sandstone. This proposal was made by George H. Worthington, a Building Committee member who was president of the Cleveland Stone Company, which would supply the material. Needless to say, he had the support of representatives from the Huntington family, who wanted all the stone supplied by their company. Yet another called for Indiana limestone over Milford granite. Sanders felt the best course was to cover the entire exterior with Georgia white marble and the interior with Ohio sandstone. Although the dispute was resolved in June for the two-tone scheme, marble over pink granite, the decision was later reconsidered.

During a ten-day on-site inspection of the marble quarries and shops, Hubbell and the contractors learned that the Georgia marble suppliers would aid the contractor in procuring stone during the winter months.[60] And, since some of the members had

Figure 41. Construction commenced on the Museum before the exterior facing material was chosen. By July 19, 1913, the foundations were being laid.

To date and to celebrate the completion of the stonework, the masons placed coins in the mortar under the capstones.

JULY 19, 1913

wanted an all-marble facade, Hubbell now held the opinion that it might be warranted from the artistic point of view. To this end, Whiting wrote to Kent asking for his opinion on an entirely marble facade—"it would cost no more"—and stated: "If you suggested it, it might give him [Hubbell] the opportunity to bring the matter before the committee comfortably." Kent agreed that "it will have to be one of the things to be regretted that it was not thought of sooner,"[61] and as a result the committee did not succumb to pressure from the Huntington heirs. An all-marble facade was approved by the Building Committee on November 17, 1913: A glistening white "temple" would sparkle in green and blue surroundings. To protect its brilliant image from the spatter of dirt, a border of sandstone was to be laid on the ground around the building.[62]

After the Museum opened in 1916, Whiting invited Huntington's children and grandchildren for a special tour in the hope that most of the antagonism over the decision favoring marble would disappear. Seeing the building, he believed, would convince them of the correctness of the final choice.[63] (Mariett Huntington, who was a Trustee, apparently did not object to the type of stone. Although she was Huntington's second wife and stepmother to his children, she apparently did not join in their crusade.)

The design and decoration of the interior spaces commanded momentous discussion. Decisions, of course, had to be made on every architectural, structural, and technical detail. While most called for pragmatic, rational conclusions based on such considerations as cost or maintenance—for instance, to have wood or bronze exterior windows (Should they open from the inside for washing?)[64]—there were several that caused heated debate and challenged prevailing ideas about what decorum dictated for a museum.

The most fervent confrontation occurred over the articulation of the Garden Court, a place envisioned as a setting for outdoor sculpture. Hubbell wanted it in white marble with Tiffany inlay like his design for the Wade Memorial Chapel in Lake View Cemetery,

whereas Kent immediately recommended[65] a rough brick finish and plants: "the cheapest brick should imply an understanding on the part of the Trustees of a commitment to purchases of Gothic and Renaissance art, which eventually should rehabilitate the place. I think that Hubbell took in the point, after seeing what Barnard had done in his marvelous little musée."[66] George G. Barnard was a New York sculptor and dealer, who had brought back medieval statuary from France, which he displayed in a small red brick, cloister-like courtyard amid the scents of flowers and incense to suggest the early Christian church (Figure 42).[67] Hubbell thought this was just dreadful.[68] With regard to the ceiling of the court Kent advised: "I would deprecate any attempt at decoration or betterment that would sacrifice the frank engineering treatment."[69] Hubbell continued to be resolutely against Kent's concept for the Garden Court, however, and Whiting also challenged it. He proposed to the Trustees that it be turned into a Persian or Indian garden with facades of old houses, stone and wood carvings, and so forth, an idea he got from Lockwood de Forest, a dealer and connoisseur of Indian art and brother of the President of the Metropolitan. At that time, Indian art was not well represented in any American museum, and it was possible to secure works of quality with little expenditure of both time and money. This idea for an instant quality collection was a plan to give individuality to the Cleveland Museum, thus enabling it to attract people from all over the United States.[70]

Whiting suggested to the Trustees that if they did not like the Indian solution, then they should have architectural fragments set in rough brick or stucco (Kent's idea). He later had doubts about this and devised a strategy for "completing" the court as "a gift from a friend." To that end, in May 1914, the Building Committee contacted New York architect Charles Platt to see if he would provide a "finished" design for the court (he was going to propose a design in the Italian Renaissance style rather than Gothic). Platt was selected because he was William G. Mather's favorite architect (he had designed Mather's Bratenahl home, Gwinn). Whiting thought that if Platt personally submitted a design to Mather that was "so attractive," the latter would donate the room. As it turned out, although Mather was willing to pay for preliminary expenses, he did not care to put any large amount of money into the Garden Court—either for architecture or for sculpture to adorn it.[71] As funds were not available for sculptures for the court, Whiting sought to locate one or two balconies and window and door frames that could be used for that purpose (given the recent earthquake in Italy, he saw an opportunity to purchase building fragments). The charges for their purchase could be made to the building account rather than against the one for acquisitions, which was then a paltry $25,000 per year. The Building Committee opposed the maneuver, although some *spolia* items were acquired this way.

In December 1914 the Building Committee considered three proposals for the Garden Court: (1) common brick walls with tile or brick walks, (2) cement walls with tiled cornice, and (3) mahogany sandstone walls. The sandstone walls were an expensive solution, $23,500; whereas the other two were nominal, around $8,000. Of the two less expensive solutions, Hubbell preferred the second (cement walls), stating that this treatment conformed with what had been carried out in both the Pan-American Building in Washington and Mrs. Jack Gardner's residence in Boston, which he believed to be the two best examples of interior courtyards in America.[72] Kelley was strongly against a brick garden court, but Bingham and Sanders voted for it solely because both Whiting and Kent recommended it;[73] while Wade voted for it, thinking it would be covered up later. He considered "a cheap brick wall" to be a mistake.[74]

In March 1915 as the brick walls were actually being constructed, Whiting demanded that construction stop and the detailing be changed. The masonry's joints, he felt, were too mechanical looking (like those on the YMCA building that Hubbell and Benes had designed) which subverted the aesthetic

Figure 42. Barnard's Cloister, New York City, served as a conceptual model for the Museum's interior Garden Court.

effect that he and Kent were seeking. Hubbell refused, demanding a direct vote and order from the Building Committee.[75] This was obtained, the walls were torn out, and a new sample was put up for the approval of Whiting and the committee: "We are following your instructions under protest, as we feel that this treatment ... will not be in harmony with the balance of the building."[76] Hubbell's protests continued as the rest of the materials for the court were decided. He wanted a Moravian, Grueby, or other "high class" tile floor; Kent, however, specified the rather commonplace Ludovici tile. Hubbell was not really opposed to the treatment itself, just to its location off the grand rotunda and to the fact that the formal, double marble staircase from the lower level terminated in it (Figure 43).[77] In the end, an unglazed red tile by Cowan, a local art pottery, was installed (and remains in part today under the loggia). Whiting recommended this tile not only on aesthetic grounds, but because Cowan gave them a special price.[78]

In 1915 a loggia was designed and its construction begun at the west end of the Garden Court.[79] As construction proceeded, the architects decided that the loggia, which they had designed, was out of scale. As a result, work was suspended while the problem was reconsidered. At first, it was decided to use lintels instead of arches above the columns.[80] To test this solution, Whiting had a small model made. Still being unsure, however, full-scale wood mockups of two alternative solutions were placed in the court itself—to see how they would actually look. After these experiments, they decided to use arches with an interior groin vaulted ceiling carried on shorter columns—a plan recommended by Benes. The architects continued to pursue a "finished" design by preparing an expansive solution with turned spindles for the loggia's balustrade.[81] In the end, four antique Roman columns were incorporated into the loggia as *spolia*, and the balustrade was simply articulated in plain brick (Figure 44).[82]

A subskylight was constructed over the Garden Court despite protests from Sanders, who felt it

Figure 43. Garden Court, looking east into the rotunda. A double stairway from the ground floor level emerged at the east end. The Garden Court also served, therefore, as a transitional area between the educational activities located on the ground floor and the main exhibition floor.

Figure 44. Garden Court, looking west. This space was designed to provide relief from museum fatigue as well as to display sculpture. Live plants, the sound of the water fountain, and the singing of birds surrounded by warm brick walls created a relaxing ambience.

Figure 45. Rotunda under construction, April 22, 1915. The walls up to the cornice level were built of stone, above that, of plaster. The rotunda was planned to serve as a nodal circulation point in the building, where visitors gather and disperse.

would give the room a much more finished appearance than was anticipated and make it more difficult to grow plants there.[83] At the last minute, in November 1915, lingering doubts were revived about the whole room, and it was almost turned into another exhibition gallery.[84]

Besides plants, birds in cages and a central fountain added the appropriate sounds to complete an inviting environment for rest, reflection, and relief from art museum fatigue. Clearly, in the design of the Garden Court cost considerations, rather than Kent's concept, played the more significant role in the decision-making process: if Mather had been willing to pay for a "finished" solution, that is what would have been built. The scarcity of money,[85] therefore, resulted in an innovative and successful solution, one that was later emulated by other museums.

Another major issue that caused a fuss was the decoration of the rotunda (Figure 45). At first, the committee pondered practical matters such as lighting and maintenance. They considered having Gutzon Borglum (who worked in the academic tradition and had received many official Washington commissions) or some other "first-class sculptor" design a circular seat with a large vase in the center containing lights to illuminate the dome. This would be supplemented by indirect lighting placed into the cornices.[86] Mrs. Huntington observed that the intended sandstone column shafts would readily soil from people pressing against them and hoped that sandstone would not be used for them. Benes went to Boston to see a chocolate-colored marble called "Charlen" used in banks there. Since it was durable and Whiting thought it would not make too big a visual contrast with the sandstone walls, it was employed for the column shafts.[87] The column capital and bases were of gray Tennessee marble, which the contractors were instructed to cut carefully and "in an artistic and spirited manner in strict accordance with models furnished by the architects."[88]

Hubbell secured a design for the dome from Tiffany Studios of New York—which proposed that it be laid with aluminum leaf decorated with an allover stencil design and glazed in colors (Figure 46).[89] They also supplied layouts for glass mosaics for decorating the lunettes, the northern wall panel, and for the rotunda walls. Whiting not only immediately came out against these proposals but in general opposed the employment of professional decorators for any inside work. He pronounced this action inappropriate and contrary to practice in museums. The interior color scheme, he declared, fell within the purview of the Museum organization. (Indeed, this was the case with McKim, Mead and White's relationship with both the Metropolitan and the Minneapolis Institute.) The committee unanimously desired sandstone for the dome itself, but specified plaster because the extra expense was not justified.[90] Despite persistent protests from Whiting, Hubbell continued to try to push the Tiffany proposals through the committee and even got them to revise their bid. As the confrontation progressed, Sanders sided with Whiting and sent a telegram to Kelley: "Tiffany ... out of harmony.... Bingham expressed opinion ... [that this is] the Museum of Art and should not be treated as ... an ordinary public building."[91] No official decision, however, was made. Later, in November 1915, the committee placed in Whiting's hands the decoration of all the exhibition galleries—subject, of course, to their approval.[92] They were growing weary and did not wish to debate every issue. In late January 1916 William A. Frances of Tiffany's wrote to Whiting inquiring about their proposal. Whiting immediately replied that he was surprised that the architects had not already informed them of the selection of a simpler scheme by the local decorator Louis Rorheimer. Frances, a friend of Whiting's, felt stabbed in the back: "[I am] greatly surprised and disappointed that ... you should have used your influence so strongly.... It is not the loss of the order[;]... we have had no advice from you or any knowledge that you would oppose us."[93] Hubbell was so keenly disappointed that he could not have the Tiffany proposals approved that he broke the committee's confidentiality. No

Figure 46. Proposed decorative scheme by Tiffany Studios for the rotunda, 1914-1915. After great debate the Building Committee decided that such a colorful and rich design was inappropriate.

Figure 47. Armor Court under construction, March 17, 1915. This stone-walled, monumentally scaled gallery is axially aligned with the rotunda and the Garden Court. While the same size as the latter, its strikingly different architectural conception provides variety within a highly ordered enfilade of spaces.

doubt he felt justified in explaining to Frances the circumstances surrounding the decision. One of Hubbell's pet schemes had been to get Wade to donate a complete Tiffany environment, but nothing ever became of it.[94]

On February 4, 1916, the committee officially decided to have each lunette in the rotunda painted and lined to look like sandstone.[95] Six days later they approved the scheme for the eye of the dome, and a yellow paint sample for the flat dome walls. Warning Hubbell, they directed: "finished walls shall be no stronger in color than the samples."[96] Whiting had obtained the advice of E. Hamilton Bell, an architect and well-known designer of theater sets and museum interiors, for this color selection and for the interior decoration of the Museum in general. (He later selected the colors for the gallery walls and designed the Museum's *Inaugural Exhibition*.) Bell advised Whiting: "I do not know your views on the interior decoration of museums, but mine are strongly in the direction of simplicity so that if you are disposed to follow my advice, you may be able to effect a considerable saving in this direction alone."[97] However, in the decision-making process there was a continual struggle between members of the Building Committee, the architects, and Whiting. While Whiting's drive for simplicity presages future developments in museum design, his ideas were not necessarily accepted by members of the Building Committee because they were viewed as ideal, but because of the reality of the project's ever-increasing cost.

The major space on the opposite side of the building from the Garden Court was designed for casts. Whiting, however, opposed purchasing casts. To persuade the Trustees that casts were passé, Whiting asked for the opinion and support of Charles L. Freer —a Detroit businessman and collector who Whiting hoped would serve as a role model for Clevelanders (he was also a member of the Museum's Advisory Council). This outside help swayed Sanders opinion,[98] which meant that the spaces previously intended for casts had to be rethought.

As Whiting's plan evolved in early 1915, serendipity played a role in developing a new concept for the court of casts.[99] One of the Museum's Trustees, Dr. Dudley P. Allen, had died in January 1915; in his memory his widow decided to donate a series of eight seventeenth-century tapestries from the Barberini Palace depicting the story of Dido and Aeneas. Of unusual quality and pedigree, they so perfectly fit the walls in the proposed court of casts that it seemed almost as if the room had been prepared for them. Serving as "splendid decorations," they helped Whiting tremendously in working out his scheme for this space as an important gallery of iron and steel work, as well as making the room one of the most splendid in the country (Figures 47 and 48).[100] To achieve Whiting's goal, John L. Severance (another Museum Trustee) and his wife donated an extensive and important collection of armor. Not only were such collections rarely seen in American museums, but its acquisition was deemed especially appropriate for industrial Cleveland, since "this would bring greater

Figure 48. The Armor Court enjoyed immediate popularity with both casual visitors and art students. It also served as the main ceremonial space in the Museum.

Figure 49. The interiors of the painting galleries were kept decidedly simple. Natural, but controlled, light illuminated the galleries from above. Oak floors were installed for the comfort of visitors.

interest to metal workers of every degree, develop their interest in art, and ever serve as a fruitful source of inspiration!"[101] On opening night the Director, Trustees, and their wives received the first Museum guests in this extraordinary gallery. The veracity of the three major trans-axial spaces—the Garden Court, rotunda, and the tapestry-lined Armor Court —was confirmed. Indeed, they remain much the same today as when the Museum opened in 1916.

Whiting believed the north galleries would be most effective if made absolutely plain rather than self-consciously decorated (Figure 49). This idea was reinforced after he read an issue of *Museumskunde* illustrating Cologne's museum, which Kent had sent to him. Furthermore, Whiting noted that simplicity would also provide the greatest possible latitude for future use.[102] (Remember, at this time Cleveland had no collection to speak of.)

To work out the details for the painting galleries, a cross sectional model was built.[103] Various flooring surfaces, from marble to cork, were considered. Ten-

nessee marble was eliminated because it would be hard on the feet, slippery, and cause a great deal of reflection in the glass of the pictures,[104] so the committee opted for Nightingale oak floors, except for the gallery directly in line with the rotunda on the north (Figure 50). Here, Whiting wanted an oak floor, as he planned to use this, the most prominently located gallery, for a colonial room to highlight early American art. The architects, however, saw the gallery as a visual continuation of the rotunda, and Kent sided with them:

I am not sure that I understand perfectly all of the questions involved in the finishing of Room IV, but it does seem to me that the architects' contention that the gallery is in a sense, a part of the Rotunda and therefore should harmonize with it (it is in vista with the Rotunda from the Entrance, is it not?) is well taken. Personally, I feel that coming between the Egyptian and Gothic rooms, as it does, it would require treatment which should serve to remind the visitor of the return to the rotunda rather than to carry the idea of a suite.[105]

Later, they decided that the borders and dados in the major galleries should be of Charlen marble while the others would have *verde terre* borders and dados.[106] The walls of the painting galleries were covered with natural-colored (a medium shade of cream or buff) monk's-cloth;[107] the results effectively eliminated any impression of coldness under artificial light at night.[108] To accommodate wheelchairs, and to provide for the smooth operation of the carts used both for moving works of art and for cleaning, all interior thresholds were eliminated.[109] To assure good lighting, the committee decided to make the appropriate decisions only after basic construction was complete so that full-scale experiments could be done *in situ*.[110]

Since the Building Committee, the mechanical engineers, and the architects all lacked particular expertise in lighting, a special committee was formed that took advantage of local talent. It was chaired by Dr. Edward P. Hyde—an able physicist of international renown who organized a research laboratory in 1908 for the study of the production of light and its effect on human welfare (now General Electric's Nela Park, East Cleveland, Ohio). The committee's task was compounded by the fact that the building was already essentially built, which added a consequential constraint to a vexing problem.[111]

At its first meeting in July 1915, the committee set precise goals to achieve quality viewing. First, the characteristics of daylight were adapted as the standard for the artificial lighting; at that time the importance of the quality of light and its influence on color was generally becoming appreciated. Second, the brightness of the floor and ceilings should not be disproportionately high in comparison with the brightness of the walls, where more light was obviously needed. Third, the downward directed light component must not be out of proportion to that directed at the walls. Fourth, any solution had to preclude reflections from glazed pictures into the eyes of observers standing at a reasonable distance.

In his efforts to find an ideal solution, Hyde in-

Figure 50. View from the south entrance looking north into the rotunda and beyond into a gallery. The architects and engineers were faced with solving the problem of how to balance the illumination levels between the different spaces that flow off the rotunda. The stone floor of the rotunda was continued in the gallery beyond to help visitors maintain their sense of orientation within the Museum as well as to sustain the formality of the entrance.

Figure 51. Attic space over a skylighted gallery. Motor-driven, adjustable louvers control the intensity and direction of the natural light. This space also contains artificial light fixtures that can be adjusted to provide the required degree of illumination below.

spected museums in New York and Boston, actually measuring lighting levels in them. By September the committee was experimenting with different lighting possibilities and had constructed a model. Later, they conducted full-scale experiments utilizing one of the actual gallery spaces.

Their biggest effort involved the design of lighting galleries from the top, in which subskylights are placed below the main skylights, forming an "attic space" in between. French and Hubbard noted how direct sunlight could be eliminated, mentioning that at Boston shades were used under the roof skylights. As this was not an effective or efficient solution, the committee decided on adjustable metal louvers—resembling jalousie windows—which were built to an original design (Figure 51).[112] Operated by electric motors controlled by conveniently located switches in the galleries below, the louvers could effectively alter the intensity of the light (which varies enormously throughout the day and year), the balance of illumi-

nation on opposite walls, and excessive downward light, and could eliminate the rake of the sunlight if operated without delay by the Museum's attendants. While seemingly a simple idea, the engineering effort required for this optimal solution was considerable—the width of the louvers, their overlap, and the distance from the skylight roof were only a few of the many variables that had to be taken into account. This louver system proved to be efficient and very inexpensive in up-keep, however, thus justifying the high initial expense.[113]

Another problem was the choice of glass for the subskylights. It could neither be transparent, since the louvers and other mechanical equipment would then be visible, nor could it be regular translucent glass, since that type of glass would diffuse the light passing through it too much and make it impossible to direct the light and to control its balance on the walls and ceilings. After much consideration, they chose an irregular crystal glass for the subskylights.

In the skylighted galleries the principal artificial light sources were located between the roof skylight and the subskylight. Special lamp holders and reflectors were designed so that they could be adjusted to the desired angular and focal position. They had to be carefully positioned both to illuminate the works of art and to eliminate bright spots on the subskylights. The light fixtures were concealed in this attic space, and the appearance of these galleries was deemed to be much finer without fixtures. Where such concealment was not possible, the fixtures chosen were made by Tiffany Studios.

During the second decade of the century lighting innovations resulted in the introduction of the tungsten bulb and the demise of the carbon filament bulb. But these vacuum bulbs blackened quickly. The first truly successful gas-filled incandescent bulb, the Mazda C-2, was commercially introduced in 1913 in large wattage (750 and 1,000) and over the next few years in wattages down to 40. The incandescent bulb was just coming into its own and the practical availability of this "daylight" artificial light source made it possible for the committee to reach its goal of having artificial illumination similar to daylight.[114]

In some galleries, such as the Armor Court, the objective was to have the subskylights uniformly bright both by day and by night. By contrast, in the Garden Court where they wanted to produce the effects of an outdoor garden at night, the lighting was accomplished by placing four lanterns on posts. Under the loggia an old lantern was electrified and placed beneath the central arch.

Great effort was also expended on the lighting design for all the other spaces, based on function and effect. In addition, the overall relationship of lighting levels between various spaces was considered; for example, what does it feel like in terms of lighting when moving between the Garden Court, rotunda, and Armor Court? Here, the committee brought a new level of sophistication to illumination design. Realizing that these spaces have a wide variance in intensity, they worked out a solution for lighting the rotunda to an average intensity and average color effect, which avoided incongruous shadows on the walls and dome. Thus, cutting edge technology and a committee of national profile that defined lighting requirements in psychological as well as pragmatic terms resulted in a noteworthy solution that set new standards for the future—Cleveland was the first large museum fully lighted by means of "artificial daylight." The committee worked without honorarium, and General Electric donated the needed 500 light bulbs.[115]

To help secure Mrs. Liberty E. Holden's collection of fourteenth- to seventeenth-century paintings for the Museum, a period room in the "Renaissance style" was decorated at the then staggering price of $15,000 (Figure 52).[116] This collection had been acquired by her late husband, Liberty E. Holden, who had served as chairman of the Building Committee. Kent was the chief negotiator with Mrs. Holden—she liked him and the attention he lavished upon her.[117] During the whole design and construction process the prospective donation was kept secret. The committee selected Arthur Loomis Harmon of New York as the designer, while the gallery's construction was entrusted to T. D. Wadelton, who had built many fine interiors.

In preparing his design, Harmon considered the possible placement of the pictures, their frames, and so forth. He took particular interest in the floor pattern (worrying that it might compete with the paintings) and in the overall color scheme, which was only decided on after the room was built.[118] During construction Whiting felt that the walls were too dark (they were covered with brown velvet fabric), but Harmon defended his design: "nothing so detracts from the complete effect of a room of that character as to get the walls too light."[119] With its vaulted ceiling enriched with ornament and color, the Holden Gallery had a strikingly different aesthetic from the other galleries.

Some of the architectural details of the Holden Gallery, such as the doorways made of artificial stone, were direct casts from the Borgia Apartments in the

Figure 52. The Holden Gallery (now modified) was decorated in a Renaissance style to secure the Holden Collection of Italian paintings. The walls, covered in brown velvet, combined with the decorative ceiling, made a marked contrast in tone and coloration with the other painting galleries. These features were considered contributory rather than exhibitory.

Vatican, while other details were based on twentieth-century interpretations of Renaissance motifs. Modern technological requirements also impinged on the design; since one air register was needed, Harmon not only had to design a grill for it but also felt compelled to install another, false one, to preserve the symmetry of his composition (they were located on the lower wall on each side of the door).[120] Electric light fixtures were installed with specifically chosen yellow globes to give the room a warm feeling. Harmon also designed the seating for the room; the stained glass windows (now in storage) were by Clement Heaton, who later did some work at Cleveland's Trinity Cathedral.

During the design stages of the Holden Gallery, Whiting was struck by the fact that the architectural doors and the false doors took up a good deal of the hanging space for paintings, which in the end turned out to be inadequate for displaying all the pictures to their best advantage.[121] Conceptually, the room itself was considered to be contributory to an aesthetic experience rather than exhibitory in its own right.[122] This gallery was subsequently remodeled when the vogue for period rooms had passed; and little remains of it today.

The 450-seat Lecture Hall had raked auditorium seating (Figure 53); its decorative scheme by the Rorheimer-Brooks Studio of Cleveland, in keeping with the major spaces in the Museum, was decidedly simple.[123] The format for the now-traditional art history lecture was already codified. A rear projection booth was provided with direct current electricity to run two slide and movie projectors and was equipped with a buzzer system connected to the front of the auditorium for notifying the projectionist.

Tucked away on the second story was space for the few casts that the Museum owned, a Photographer's Studio (Figure 54), and an 85-by-33-foot Children's Museum. Located away from the areas designed for adults, "little people," as the periodical *Outlook* reported, "may find such objects as interest them ... without disturbing their elders by excited prattle, the necessary expression of a child's eager interest."[124]

Figure 53. Lecture Hall (now destroyed). From the beginning a lecture hall or auditorium was considered necessary to the educational mission of the Museum. It was equipped with both movie and slide projectors.

Figure 54. The Photographer's Studio was located in the second floor attic to take advantage of the natural light from the skylights.

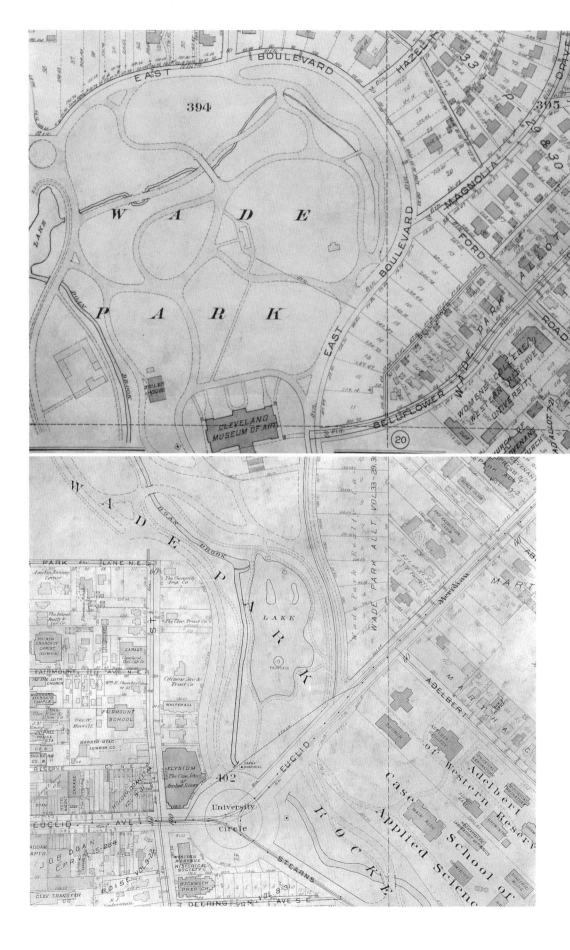

Figure 55. Site plan, as built, showing the relationship of the Museum to Euclid Avenue and the location of the Boiler House. This plan predates the final landscaping of the area in front of the Museum.

Figure 56. A Boiler House (now destroyed) was built to provide steam in the summer season, when the supply from the city was shut off.

(Natural science items were also included. The idea for an adjoining natural history museum dates to this time. Furthermore, a stand-alone Children's Museum was designed by Walker and Weeks, though not built, in the 1920s.)

The choice of mechanical systems for the building was based on the latest experiments, circumstances and conditions particular to Cleveland, and cost-benefit analyses. From the beginning Mayor Newton D. Baker agreed to provide an adjacent site for a power facility. It was soon discovered, however, that steam could be supplied directly by the city from a nearby plant. The cost of construction of the power plant was thus saved—it was put into other parts of the building—and the environment of the park was protected from smoke and dust. This solution seemed ideal. However, in December 1914, the engineers wrote Whiting that steam was necessary for dehumidification in the summertime. But the city, it was discovered, could not supply steam then. The idea for a small, auxiliary plant in the building itself was dismissed for technical (coal dust would hurt the exhibits) and aesthetic reasons—the building code required that the chimney be at least 16 feet above the marble coping and the city would not grant a variance. Such a chimney would have been visually incongruous with the building. To pay for this plant, the Huntington Trustees made an additional fiscal commitment.[125] In December 1916, after protracted negotiations, City Council provided the land for a boiler plant on the hillside west of the building (Figures 55 and 56); Wade also gave his reversionary rights for the property to the Museum.[126] Its design and construction took most of 1917 and 1918. The Museum did a cost-benefit analysis to determine if electric power should be purchased from the Cleveland Electric Illuminating Company or from the city's newly opened Municipal Light plant (called Muny Light then and Cleveland Public Power now), which was the largest municipally owned generating plant in the nation.[127]

After considerable debate, automatic thermostats were installed to control the heat in the winter. Al-

though of questionable reliability at that time, they had been used for eight years at Boston and were universally liked by the employees there.[128] To protect the works of art from damage, water spray air washers capable of removing 98 percent of the dirt and foreign matter entering the air were installed; so that dirt would not be recirculated in the air, the building was equipped with a built-in central vacuum cleaner.

Two gigantic, 8- and 10-foot, motor-driven fans, capable of moving up to 24,000 and 41,000 cubic feet of air per minute respectively, were placed in the basement to draw fresh air into the building through two separate duct networks (Figure 57). The air intakes, which open out on the roof, were located on either side of the south entrance. (These original fans are still in operation today.) The rationale for two systems was quite simple. One served the main gallery floor, where it was essential to maintain a different temperature and humidity to safeguard the objects on exhibition than on the lower level and second floor areas, which had other uses. Foul air was removed

from the second floor and lower level by gravity vent ducts. By contrast, from the gallery level it was drawn by a fan and discharged through a roof outlet. When the number of people in the galleries was small and fresh air was not required, the air could be recirculated. The proportion of fresh to recirculated air was regulated by dampers operated by the pneumatic switches installed in the duct work. To maintain a constant temperature and humidity in the galleries, the air was circulated twenty-four hours a day, and a hygrostat, located in the return air duct from the galleries, controlled the humidification equipment. Besides being cleaned and humidified, outside air was automatically preheated to increase comfort as well as to control humidity and to reduce overall heating expenses.[129]

One of the Museum's major environmental problems was minimizing the heat that naturally accompanied the sought-after light coming in through the skylights. To this end, a recirculating water system was built to produce a thin layer of moisture by way of spraying water on the outside of the skylight glass to cool it in the summertime. The fact that the spray nozzles themselves were given artistic form did not seem to affect their efficacy (Figure 58); in 1917 very little difference could be measured when the roof was being sprayed with water (about a 2 percent reduction). Since the building itself is a heavy masonry structure (the outer walls are stone over a brick core), it naturally retains its nighttime coolness well into the next day; the inside-outside temperature differential averaged 10 and 13 degrees.[130] The water sprays had one other function: washing the skylights (Figure 59). To rid the skylight area of heat in the summer and moisture in the winter, automatic dampers were installed. Likewise, steam pipes were installed to melt the snow which accumulated on the skylights in winter—blocking the light and placing a dangerously heavy load on the glass. Despite these innovations, problems were apparent after the building opened, the major ones being leaking skylights and climate

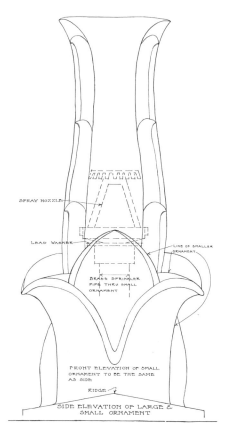

Figure 58. Bronze water spray nozzles were located on the roof to provide a fine mist of water to cool the skylight glass. They were part of an overall strategy to maintain even temperatures in the galleries below. Hubbell and Benes, drawing.

Figure 59. The ridges of the skylights on the roof are decorated with ornamental cresting.

control. Complete climate control, however, was just in its infancy at that time, and French and Hubbard were investigating the installation of ammonia pipes for cooling and dehumidification at Filene's Department Store in Boston; since it required a 150 horsepower refrigerating apparatus to make it work, the solution was very expensive.[131] (Until recent times, to cool the air on special occasions when the Museum has had an extraordinarily large number of visitors, tons of ice were actually placed in the 8- and 10-foot fan chambers.)

Realizing that efficient communication was the *sine qua non* of modern business, Whiting decided to install sixteen Bell telephones for the Museum staff, and two pay Bell telephones, as well as two pay Cuyahoga stations—which served different parts of the region—for patrons.[132]

The mechanical and technical details, as well as the Museum's interior design, took well over four years to resolve. To save time—the Attorney General's suits persisted into 1915—most decisions were made in the course of actual construction. Today, this way of building is called "fast-tracking." In the end, numerous problems, many of which were never fully foreseen by the Trustees, had to be overcome: the unification of purpose, the arrangement of the site, the definition of the programmatic needs of a museum, and the design of the structure itself. The end result was, however, a remarkably modern and fine building set amongst the leaves of Wade Park.

Of course, a building alone does not make a museum (Figure 60). Museums are essentially for use, and it is through the fulfillment of function that they attain relevance. As Albert Ryder noted in an article on Cleveland's Museum in the *American Magazine of Art* in 1916: "There is something raw and chilly about a new museum, up the stairs of which but few feet have tramped and through the halls of which almost no seekers after pleasure and knowledge have wandered. The atmosphere is lacking, but the sense of undeveloped opportunities and possibilities is great."[133] Innovative programming and a thoughtful acquisitions policy alone, however, cannot account for The Cleveland Museum of Art's emergence as a world-class institution. Its architectural image contributed to its acceptance, stature, and support by the greater Cleveland community. When it opened to the public on June 7, 1916, Clevelanders knew they had an Art Museum. The thirty-year struggle for its birth was immediately forgotten.

Figure 60. To the present day, the south facade remains the Museum's trademark. The landscaping was completed in 1928 after a design by the Olmsted Brothers, landscape architects, Boston, with the cooperation of the Cleveland Garden Center (now The Garden Center of Greater Cleveland), the Museum, private donors, and the City of Cleveland.

1. Hubbell and Benes to Fuller, July 12, 1910, 1916 Building file, Corporate, CMA Archives. These figures were later given by Hermon Kelley, see *Cleveland Leader*, July 20, 1911.

2. Minutes of the John Huntington Art and Polytechnic Trust, June 7, 1911, CMA Archives. Sanders was requested to continue his search and make recommendations. Early the next year Hubbell wrote to Sanders asking for instructions, pointing out that no instructions had been received since July 1910. Hubbell to Sanders, February 16, 1911, W. B. Sanders file, 1909-1913, Harold T. Clark Papers, CMA Archives.

3. Minutes of the Cleveland Museum of Art [now the Horace Kelley Art Foundation], September 6, 1910, Record Book no. 2. The delegation consisted of Hatch, J. G. W. Cowles, and Kelley. At that meeting, Kelley informed the Trustees that the Cleveland Museum of Art had $350,000 in cash. He felt that they should spend no more than $250,000 on the building, leaving $100,000 to defray operating expenses. At the time, this corporation had other assets, i.e., land, which they were apparently unwilling to sell. For the letter to Rockefeller, see Corporate, CMA Archives.

4. Minutes of the Cleveland Museum of Art [now the Horace Kelley Art Foundation], April 5, 1911, Record Book no. 2.

5. Cleveland, *City Council Proceedings*, file no. 20141, January 30, 1911, and file no. 20618, March 13, 1911; *Cleveland Plain Dealer*, January 24, 1911.

6. *Cleveland Plain Dealer*, May 29, 1911.

7. Ibid., July 12, 1911; During this period Record Book no. 2 of the Cleveland Museum of Art [now the Horace Kelley Art Foundation] substantiates the newspaper's claim that it was difficult to achieve a quorum at meetings.

8. Ibid., May 29, 1911. Two suits were actually filed. One against the Trustees of the Hurlbut estate, the other against the Trustees of the Cleveland Museum of Art [now the Horace Kelley Art Foundation]. Cuyahoga Court of Common Pleas, nos. 125082/3, Appearance Docket 247; *Cleveland Plain Dealer*, July 12, 1911.

9. *Cleveland Leader*, July 12, 1911.

10. Ibid., July 13, 1911. The committee consisted of banker F. H. Goff, architect B. S. Hubbell, and the secretary of the chamber Munson Havens.

11. Minutes of the Cleveland Museum of Art [now the Horace Kelley Art Foundation], June 15, 1911, Record Book no. 2. They appointed Wade, McNairy, and Kelley.

12. Minutes of the Board of Trustees of the Cleveland Museum of Art [now the Horace Kelley Art Foundation], June 19, 27, 1911; Perkins to Kelley, June 12, 1911, Record Book no. 2; Minutes of the John Huntington Art and Polytechnic Trust, June 7, 1911; Sanders to Perkins, June 21, 1911, W. B. Sanders file, 1909-1913, Harold T. Clark Papers, The lease was drawn up in 1912, and Hubbell and Benes prepared the drawing and legal description. Drawing, January 16, 1912, Lease, May 3, 1912, Corporate, CMA Archives. The lease is recorded in the Record of Leases, June 19, 1914, and vol. 48, p. 20 of Maps, Cuyahoga County.

13. Minutes of the John Huntington Art and Polytechnic Trust, July 3, 1911, CMA Archives; Minutes of the Cleveland Museum of Art [now the Horace Kelley Art Foundation], Record Book no. 2, July 26, 1911.

14. Henry W. Kent, Henry W. Kent file (9-12-64), Harold T. Clark Papers, J. H. Wade to Sanders, September 9, 1911; Sage to Sanders, October 17, 1912; Secretary of the Board Huntington Art and Polytechnic Trust to Kent confirming the Building Committee's offer, November 26, 1911; Sanders to Kent, November 28, 1911, urging Kent to accept the offer; Sanders to Kent, January 2, 1912 (*actually typed*, however, 1911), Kent indicates his willingness to come for a month to supervise the work of the architects; Whiting to Sanders, January 27, 1913, in which he accepts the job as Director, W. B. Sanders file, 1909-1913, Harold T. Clark Papers, CMA Archives.

15. Minutes of the Building Committee, July 3, 1911; Minutes of the John Huntington Art and Polytechnic Trust, July 25, 1911, CMA Archives; Minutes, Cleveland Museum of Art [now the Horace Kelley Art Foundation], July 26, 1911, Record Book no. 2; *Cleveland Plain Dealer*, July 27, 1911. The *Cleveland Plain Dealer* reported that this solution was first proposed by the Kelley Foundation.

16. The architects developed five different proposals for dividing up the ownership of the remaining three quadrants of the building. See, for example, Hubbell and Benes to H. A. Kelley, December 6 and 31, 1910, Records of the Building Committee, Corporate, CMA Archives.

17. *Cleveland Plain Dealer*, July 27, 1911.

18. *Cleveland Leader*, July 27, 1911.

19. Minutes of the Cleveland Museum of Art [now the Horace Kelley Art Foundation], Record Book no. 2, September 6, 1910.

20. These visual solutions had been articulated much earlier in 1910. See *Cleveland Plain Dealer*, July 11, 1910.

21. Record Book of the Building Committee, Memorandum, October 30, 1911, Corporate, CMA Archives.

22. Minutes of the Building Committee, November 10, 1911, Corporate, CMA Archives.

23. Memorandum, November 17, 1911, Records of the Building Committee, Corporate, CMA Archives.

24. Memorandum, November 17, 1911, Records of the Building Committee, CMA Archives; Minutes of the Cleveland Museum of Art [now the Horace Kelley Art Foundation], December 2, 1911. The approved plan bears the date November 16, 1911.

25. Minutes of the Cleveland Museum of Art [now the Horace Kelley Art Foundation], December 2, 1911, Record Book no. 2. The Trustees recognized that these new developments were causing great real estate activity in the area, they received an offer to purchase their property on Superior. They did not sell, but referred the matter to the Real Estate Committee for advice.

26. Otto Wagner, translated from the German by N. Clifford Ricker, "Modern Architecture," *The Brickbuilder* 10 (1901): 144. This was published under the auspices of the Architectural League of America, of which Hubbell was a member.

27. "The Albright Art Gallery," *Academy Notes* 1, 1 (June 1905): 3.

28. Eugène E. Viollet-le-Duc, *Discourses on Architecture*, trans. Benjamin Bucknall (Boston: Ticknor and Co., 1889), 1: 61. Hubbell would have known this book.

29. "The Albright Art Gallery," 3.

30. *Dialogo di pittura* (Venice, 1548). Quoted in *Encyclopedia of World Art* (1961), 4: 539.

31. Minutes of the Building Committee, June 18, 1915, Corporate, CMA Archives. The idea to delete the inscription goes back to 1913 and was Kent's. Kent to Sanders, April 19, 1913, file 874, H. W. Kent/C. F. Bingham, Director Whiting (I), CMA Archives.

32. Minutes of the Building Committee, March 29, 1916, Corporate, CMA Archives.

33. Wagner, "Modern Architecture," 171.

34. Besides appearing in local newspapers this scheme was published in the architectural press, see "Cleveland Museum of Art: Model of Proposed Structure Gives Earnest of Early Fulfillment of Long Deferred Hopes," *The Ohio Architect and Builder* 20, 5 (November 1912): 70-71.

35. *Cleveland Plain Dealer*, November 15, 1912.

36. *Cleveland Leader*, November 15, 1912.

37. *Cleveland Plain Dealer*, November 15, 1912.

38. The Cleveland Museum of Art, *The New Building in Wade Park* (Cleveland: Horace Carr, 1912). Copy in Corporate, CMA Archives.

39. W. B. Sanders file, 1909-1913, Harold T. Clark Papers, CMA Archives. The file contains many letters written in 1912 to George B. Harris and Joseph Hidy, who handled the state's case.

40. Sanders to Hubbell and Benes, September 3, 1912, W. B. Sanders file, 1909-1913, Harold T. Clark Papers, CMA Archives.

41. Memorandum, November 9, 1936, based on a conversation with Kent on July 5, 1936, Henry W. Kent file (9-12-64), Harold T. Clark Papers, CMA Archives.

42. Henry W. Kent, "Business Methods in the Metropolitan Museum of Art," *Bulletin of the Metropolitan Museum of Art* 6 (January 1912): 169-170.

43. Hubbell to Bingham, October 22, 1912, C. W. Bingham, file 137, Director Whiting (I), CMA Archives.

44. Minutes of the Building Committee Meeting, November 6, 1912, Corporate, CMA Archives.

45. Minutes of the Building Committee, April 24, 1913, Corporate, CMA Archives.

46. Sanders to Kent, March 20, 1913, W. B. Sanders, 1909-1913, Harold T. Clark Papers, CMA Archives.

47. Hubbell to CMA Building Committee, October 24, 1913, Hubbell and Benes, file 147, Director Whiting (I), CMA Archives.

48. *The Classified Business and Directors Directory*, 7th ed. (Cleveland: Penton Press Co., 1913), 669.

49. Kelley to Sanders, April 9, 1913; Sanders to Kelley, April 26, 1913, W. B. Sanders file, 1909-1913, Harold T. Clark Papers, CMA Archives.

50. Minutes of the John Huntington Art and Polytechnic Trust, May 5, 1913. The contract between the company and the trusts bears the date May 21, 1913, see Constitution, by-laws, 1913-14, W. B. Sanders file, Harold T. Clark Papers, and Corporate, Crowell and Sherman Contract, CMA Archives.

51. CMA Archives.

52. Minutes of the Building Committee, December 18, 1919, Corporate, CMA Archives.

53. Sanders to Kelley, February 27, 1912, W. B. Sanders file, 1909-1913, Harold T. Clark Papers, CMA Archives.

54. Kelley to Sanders, April 24, 1912, W. B. Sanders file, 1909-1913, Harold T. Clark Papers, CMA Archives.

55. Sanders to Kelley, April 5, 1913, W. B. Sanders file, 1909-1913, Harold T. Clark Papers, CMA Archives.

56. Sanders to Kelley, April 25, 1913, W. B. Sanders file, 1909-1913, Harold T. Clark Papers, CMA Archives.

57. Minutes of the John Huntington Art and Polytechnic Trust, May 5, 1913, and Minutes of the Building Committee, May 6, 1913, CMA Archives.

58. Board Minutes [new], vol. 1, Corporate; Whiting to Sanders, December 24, 1913, W. B. Sanders, file 132, Director Whiting (I); Agreement, Cleveland Museum of Art [new], John Huntington Art and Polytechnic Trust and Horace Kelley Art Foundation, January 27, 1914; Supplemental Agreement, October 30, 1929, Corporate, CMA Archives.

59. Minutes of the Building Committee, June 9, 1913, Corporate, CMA Archives.

60. Hubbell and Benes and Crowell and Sherman Co., "Report to the Building Committee to Granite and Marble Quarries and Shops, October 13, 1913," Hubbell and Benes, file 147, Director Whiting (I), CMA Archives. The trip took place September 18-28, 1913.

61. Whiting to Kent, October 17, 1913; Kent to Whiting, October 20, 1913; Metropolitan Museum of Art, Kent, file 1, Director Whiting (I), CMA Archives.

62. Minutes of the Building Committee, October 25 and November 4, 1915, Corporate, CMA Archives.

63. Whiting to Wade, June 24, 1916, J. H. Wade, file 134, Director Whiting (I), CMA Archives.

64. Minutes of the Building Committee, June 11, 1914, Corporate, CMA Archives.

65. Memorandum, November 9, 1936, interview with Kent, Kent file, Harold T. Clark Papers, CMA Archives.

66. Kent to Whiting, January 2, 1914, Metropolitan Museum of Art, Henry W. Kent, file 1, Director Whiting (I), CMA Archives.

67. Winifred E. Howe, *A History of the Metropolitan Museum of Art*, 2 vols. (New York, 1946), 2: 210.

68. Whiting to Kent, January 6, 1915, Metropolitan Museum of Art, Kent file 1, Director Whiting (I), CMA Archives.

69. Kent to Sanders, June 16, 1913, Kent-Bingham, file 874, Director Whiting (I), CMA Archives.

70. "To the Trustees, January 6, 1914," Reports, Director Whiting (II). On June 30, 1914, Kent wrote to Whiting: "plain brick walls and skylight originally planned would not seem to me so bad a fate as I fear you think it." Metropolitan Museum of Art, Henry W. Kent, file 1, Director Whiting (I), CMA Archives.

71. Whiting to Kent, May 7, 1914; Kent to Whiting, May 9, 1914; Whiting to Kent, May 27, 1914; and Whiting to Kent, June 27, 1914, Metropolitan Museum of Art, Henry W. Kent, file 1, Director Whiting (I). Minutes of the Building Committee, May 3, June 11, 1914, Corporate. Whiting did not give up easily. Hoping still to interest Mather, he and Mather visited Barnard. Whiting to Barnard, February 2, 1915, Barnard, file 242, Director Whiting (I), CMA Archives.

72. Hubbell to Whiting, February 3, 1915, Hubbell and Benes, file 147, Director Whiting (I), CMA Archives.

73. Whiting to Kent, December 14, 1914, file 1, Metropolitan Museum of Art, Henry W. Kent, Director Whiting (I), CMA Archives.

74. Minutes of the Building Committee, March 6, 1915, Corporate, CMA Archives.

75. Whiting to Bingham, dayletter, March 6, 1915, W. C. Bingham, file 137, Director Whiting (I), CMA Archives.

76. Hubbell to the Committee, March 8, 1915, Records of the Building Committee, Corporate, CMA Archives.

77. Minutes of the Building Committee, June 18, 1915, Corporate, CMA Archives.

78. Whiting to Hubbell and Benes, September 3, 1915, Hubbell and Benes, file 147, Director Whiting (I); Minutes of the Building Committee, November 4, 1915, Corporate, CMA Archives.

79. Minutes of the Building Committee, August 30, 1915, Corporate, CMA Archives.

80. Minutes of the Building Committee, November 4, 1915, CMA Archives.

81. Minutes of the Building Committee, November 18, 1915, CMA Archives.

82. Hubbell asked the committee to approve the final design on December 2, 1915. Minutes of the Building Committee, December 2, 1915; Hubbell to the committee, December 2, 1915, Records of the Building Committee, Corporate, CMA Archives.

83. Minutes of the Building Committee, November 16, 1915, Corporate, CMA Archives.

84. Whiting to Hubbell, November 6, 1915: "hold off on ordering tile, perhaps Garden Court with subskylight will be turned into an exhibition gallery." Hubbell and Benes, file 147, Director Whiting (I), CMA Archives.

85. Funds, in fact, were so restricted that Bingham told Whiting that it might be impossible to not only finish the court, but also the north galleries. See Whiting to Kent, October 26, 1914, Metropolitan Museum of Art, Henry W. Kent, file 1, Director Whiting (I), CMA Archives.

86. Minutes of the Building Committee, October 21, 1914, Corporate, CMA Archives.

87. Minutes of Building Committee, November 3, 1914; Whiting to Kent, September 30, 1914, in which he mentions Mrs. Huntington's contribution and asks Kent for his advice, Metropolitan Museum of Art, Henry W. Kent, file 1, Director Whiting (I), CMA Archives.

88. Original Specifications, Marble Revision #1, November 28, 1914, 1916 Building file, Corporate, CMA Archives.

89. Decorating Estimate, October 15, 1915, Tiffany Studios, file 486, Director Whiting (I), CMA Archives.

90. Minutes of the Building Committee, October 11, 1915, Corporate, CMA Archives.

91. Minutes of the Building Committee, October 18, 1915, Corporate, CMA Archives.

92. Minutes of the Building Committee, November 4, 1915, Corporate, CMA Archives.

93. William A. Frances, Tiffany Studios to Whiting, January 31, 1916; Frances to Whiting, February 5, 1916; Whiting to Frances, February 8, 1916, Tiffany Studios, file 486, Director Whiting (I), CMA Archives.

94. Whiting to Kent, July 29, 1915, Metropolitan Museum of Art, Henry W. Kent, file 1, Director Whiting (I), CMA Archives.

95. Minutes of the Building Committee, February 4, 1916, Corporate, CMA Archives.

96. Minutes of the Building Committee, February 10, 1916, Corporate, CMA Archives.

97. Whiting to Bell, December 20, 1915; Bell to Whiting, December 23, 1915; and Whiting to Bell, January 13, 1916, Hamilton Bell, file 873, Director Whiting (I), CMA Archives.

98. Whiting to Sanders, July 6, 1915, W. B. Sanders, file 132, Director Whiting (I), CMA Archives.

99. Whiting to Kent, February 18, 1915: "court of casts now a gallery of iron work, armor, etc., as I have now under consideration following a talk with Mr. Mather," Holden Gallery, file 607, Director Whiting (I), CMA Archives.

100. Whiting to Sanders, March 10, 12, 1915, W. B. Sanders, file 132, Director Whiting (I), CMA Archives.

101. The Cleveland Museum of Art, *Catalogue of the Inaugural Exhibition, June 6-September 20, 1916* (Cleveland, 1916), 234.

102. Whiting to Kent, October 20, 1914, Metropolitan Museum of Art, Henry W. Kent, file 1, Director Whiting (I), CMA Archives.

103. Minutes of the Building Committee, January 23, 1914, Corporate, CMA Archives.

104. Whiting to Kent, October 29, 1914, Metropolitan Museum of Art, Henry W. Kent, file 1, Director Whiting (I), CMA Archives.

105. Whiting to Kent, April 20, 23, 1915; Kent to Whiting, April 25, 1915, Metropolitan Museum of Art, Henry W. Kent, file 1, Director Whiting (I), CMA Archives.

106. Minutes of the Building Committee, March 1, 1915, Corporate, CMA Archives.

107. Estimate signed by W. J. Kohler, August 30, 1915, Louis Rorheimer, file 306, Director Whiting (I), CMA Archives.

108. E. P. Hyde, "Lighting of the Cleveland Museum of Art," *Illuminating Engineering Society, Transactions* 11 (1916): 1037.

109. Whiting to Harmon, June 16, 1915, Holden Gallery, file 607, Director Whiting (I), CMA Archives.

110. Minutes of the Building Committee, February 26, 1915, Corporate, CMA Archives.

111. The members of the committee besides Hyde were W. V. Batson, S. E. Doane, E. J. Edwards, Ward Harrison, M. Luckiesh, J. A. MacLean, W. R. McCornack, and F. A. Whiting. The following discussion is taken from its final report "Lighting of the Cleveland Museum of Art," 1014-1041.

112. French and Hubbard to Whiting, October 4, 14, 1915, French and Hubbard, file 124, Director Whiting (I), CMA Archives.

113. Whiting to Bradford Boardman, Executive Assistant, Metropolitan Museum of Art, May 20, 1929, Lighting Committee Reports, file 368b, Director Whiting (I), CMA Archives.

114. Paul W. Keating, *Lamps for a Brighter America, A History of the General Electric Lamp Business* (New York: McGraw-Hill Book Company, 1954), 75-79, 112-114.

115. Minutes of the Building Committee, December 23, 1915, Corporate, CMA Archives.

116. The Museum clearly did this to obtain the donation. See Whiting to Kent, March 31, 1914, Metropolitan Museum of Art, Henry W. Kent, file 1, Director Whiting (I), CMA Archives.

117. Whiting to Kent, June 4, 1914, Director Whiting (I), CMA Archives.

118. Harmon to Whiting, November 4, 1915; drawing scale 1/4 inch to 1 foot, showing hanging scheme for the paintings, Holden Gallery, file 607, Director Whiting (I), CMA Archives.

119. Harmon to Whiting, December 20, 1915, Holden Gallery, file 607, Director Whiting (I), CMA Archives.

120. Harmon to Whiting, June 17, 1915, Holden Gallery, file 607, Director Whiting (I), CMA Archives.

121. Whiting to Kent, March 27, 1915, Metropolitan Museum of Art, Henry W. Kent, file 1, Director Whiting (I), CMA Archives.

122. Kent to Whiting, August 11, 1915, Metropolitan Museum of Art, Henry W. Kent, file 1, Director Whiting (I), CMA Archives.

123. Minutes of the Building Committee, November 16, 1915, Corporate, CMA Archives.

124. "The Cleveland Museum of Art," *Outlook* 113 (14 June 1916): 349.

125. Recalled in Hubbard to Whiting, March 10, 1915, Hubbard to Whiting, December 19, 1914; and Hubbard to Hubbell and Benes, March 8, 1915, French and Hubbard, file 124, Director Whiting (I); Minutes of the Building Committee, August 2, 1915, Corporate, CMA Archives.

126. December 1916. The negotiations with the city were conducted by Hubbell. Earlier on July 21, 1915, Mayor Baker said a plant in this location was out of the question; it was not approved until Harry L. Davis was mayor. See "Report to Mr. Charles W. Bingham on Methods of Obtaining Auxiliary Heat at Bi-Party Building." July 1915, 1916 Building file, Corporate, CMA Archives.

127. Whiting to Hubbell and Benes, October 15, 1914, file 147, Hubbell and Benes, Director Whiting (I), CMA Archives.

128. Whiting to Bingham, January 29, 1915, C. W. Bingham, file 137, Director Whiting (I), CMA Archives.

129. Original Specifications, 1916 Building file, Corporate; "Description of, and directions for, running the heating system, 2-25-1916," French and Hubbard, file 503, Director Whiting (I), CMA Archives.

130. Whiting to Kent, August 7, 1917, Holden Gallery, file 607, Director Whiting (I); "Record of Gallery Temperature Readings with Roof Sprays in Operation, August 14 to September 22, 1917," CMA Archives.

131. French and Hubbard to Whiting, July 24, 1916, French and Hubbard, file 124, Director Whiting (I), CMA Archives.

132. Whiting to Hubbard, March 13, 1915, file 124, Director Whiting (I), CMA Archives.

133. Albert Ryder, "The New Cleveland Museum of Art," *American Magazine of Art* 7, 10 (August 1916): 395.

SELECTED BIBLIOGRAPHY

Manuscript Sources

Boston, Massachusetts. Museum of Fine Arts. Archival Collection.

Boston Public Library. Wheelwright, Haven & Holt Collection.

Massachusetts Historical Society. Henry W. Bellows Papers. Wheelwright Family Papers.

Cleveland, Ohio. City Council Archives.

Cleveland Museum of Art. Archives.

Cleveland Museum of Natural History. Archives.

Cuyahoga County Archives. Probate Court Records.

Cuyahoga County Court House. Court of Common Pleas, Records. Court of Insolvency, Records.

Western Reserve Historical Society. Archives. American Institute of Architects, Cleveland Chapter, Minutes. Newton D. Baker Papers. Cleveland Chamber of Commerce, Records. Wallace H. Cathcart Papers. Tom L. Johnson Papers. Hermon A. Kelley Papers. Wade Family Papers.

Published Sources

"The Albright Art Gallery." *Academy Notes* 1, 1 (June 1905): 3-5.

"Architects for Museum." *The Ohio Architect and Builder* 8, 4 (October 1906): 41.

The Biographical Cyclopaedia and Portrait Gallery with an Historical Sketch of the State of Ohio. Cincinnati: Western Biographical Publishing Co., 1883-1894.

Bolton, Charles Edward. *A Few Civic Problems of Greater Cleveland.* Cleveland, 1897.

Brewer, Cecil Claude. "American Museum Buildings." *Journal of the Royal Institute of British Architects*, 3rd series, 20 (1913): 365-403.

"Build the Museum Down Town." *The Ohio Architect and Builder* 1, 6 (June 1903): 4.

Burcaw, George Ellis. *Introduction to Museum Work.* Nashville: American Association for State and Local History, 1975.

Cantor, Jay. "Temples of the Arts: Museum Architecture in Nineteenth-Century America." *Bulletin of the Metropolitan Museum of Art* 28, 8 (April 1970): 331-354.

Catalogue of the Architectural Exhibition of the Cleveland Architectural Club. Cleveland: The Caxton Co., 1909.

The Classified Business and Directors Directory. 7th Edition. Cleveland: Penton Press Co., 1913.

Cleveland, Ohio. *City Council Proceedings.*

Cleveland, Ohio. *List of Streets Accepted by Ordinances, Deed, etc., to June 1, 1900.* Cleveland, 1900.

Cleveland Museum of Art. *Catalogue of the Inaugural Exhibition, June 6-September 20, 1916.* Cleveland: The Cleveland Museum of Art, 1916.

———. *New Building in Wade Park.* Cleveland: Horace Carr, 1912.

"Cleveland Museum of Art." *Architecture and Building* 48 (August 1916): 140-144.

"Cleveland Museum of Art." *The Ohio Architect and Builder* 20, 5 (November 1912): 70-71.

"Cleveland Museum of Art." *Outlook* 113 (June 14, 1916): 349.

"Cleveland Museum of Art As It Looks Today." *The Ohio Architect and Builder* 25, 4 (April 1915): 33-34.

Coleman, Laurence Vail. *Museum Buildings.* Vol. 1: *A Planning Study.* Washington, DC: American Association of Museums, 1950.

Conway, William Martin. *The Domain of Art.* New York: Dutton, 1902.

Cox, Kenyon. *A Public Policy of an Art Gallery in America* [Address before the Cleveland Chamber of Commerce, October 10, 1906]. Cleveland: 1906.

Dana, John Cotton. *The New Museum.* Woodstock, VT: The Elm Tree Press, 1917.

———. *New Relations of Museums and Industries.* Newark, NJ: The Newark Museum Association, 1919.

Daneker, Jermone G. *The Romance of Georgia Marble.* Baltimore and New York: Thomsen-Ellis Co., 1927.

"Edmund March Wheelwright, '76." *The Harvard Graduates' Magazine* 21 (December 1912): 240-242.

Ferree, Barr. "Museum Building and Arrangement." *Engineering Magazine* 2 (October 1891-March 1892): 221-237.

Frary, Ihna T. "The Cleveland Museum of Art." *Architectural Record* 40, 3 (September 1916): 194-211.

Georgia Marble Co. *Architects Service Catalog.* n.d.

"Get the Art Museum." *The Ohio Architect and Builder* 16, 1 (July 1910): 11.

Gilder, Richard Watson. Poem: "A Temple of Art." [Written for the opening of the Albright Art Gallery] In *The Critic* 47 (1905): 154-155.

Gilman, Benjamin Ives. *Museum Ideals of Purpose and Method.* Cambridge, MA: Harvard University Press, 1923.

"A Great Museum of Art." *The Ohio Architect and Builder* 5, 6 (June 1905): 33.

Heckscher, Morrison H. "Hunt and the Metropolitan Museum of Art." In *The Architecture of Richard Morris Hunt.* Edited by Susan R. Stein. Chicago: University of Chicago Press, 1986.

Henry Wood Elliott, 1846-1930: A Retrospective Exhibition. Anchorage: Anchorage Historical and Fine Arts Museum, 1982.

Howe, Winifred E. *A History of the Metropolitan Museum of Art.* 2 vols. New York: The Metropolitan Museum of Art, 1913-1946.

Hubbell, Benjamin S. "Building an Art Museum." *The Cornell Architect* 2, 1 (February 1916): 3-6.

———. "The Cleveland Museum of Art." *Journal of the Cleveland Engineering Society* 6 (November 1913): 168-179.

Hyde, Edward P. "Lighting of the Cleveland Museum of Art." *Illuminating Engineering Society. Transactions* 11 (1916): 1014-1041.

Ingham, Mary Bigelow James. *Women of Cleveland and Their Work.* Cleveland: W. A. Ingham, 1893.

Johannesen, Eric. *Cleveland Architecture, 1876-1976.* Cleveland: The Western Reserve Historical Society, 1979.

Johnson, Homer H. "Cleveland's Opportunity in Art." *The Ohio Architect and Builder* 7, 6 (June 1906): 13-20.

Keating, Paul W. *Lamps for a Brighter America, A History of the General Electric Lamp Business.* New York: McGraw-Hill Book Co., 1954.

Kelley, Hermon A. "The Growth of Cleveland as an Art Center." *Art and Archaeology* 16, 4-5 (October-November 1923): 131-133.

Kent, Henry W. "Business Methods in the Metropolitan Museum of Art." *Bulletin of the Metropolitan Museum of Art* 6 (January 1911): 169-170.

————. "Museums of Art." *Architectural Forum* 47 (December 1927): 581-600.

————. "The Small Museum." *Art and Progress* 4, 10 (August 1913): 1047-1056.

————. *What I am Pleased to Call My Education.* Edited by Lois Leighton Comings. New York: The Grolier Club, 1949.

————. "The Why and Wherefore of Museum Planning." *Architectural Forum* 56, 6 (June 1932): 529-532.

Kurtz, Charles. "The Albright Art Gallery of Buffalo, New York." *International Studio (N. Y.)* 26 (1905): xxxv-xxxix.

Leedy, Jr.,Walter C. "Cleveland's Struggle for Self-Identity." In *Modern Architecture in America: Visions and Revisions.* Edited by Richard Guy Wilson and Sidney K. Robinson, 74-105. Ames: Iowa State University Press, 1991.

Lewis, Joanne M. *To Market To Market: An Old-Fashioned Family Story: The West Side Market.* Cleveland Heights, OH: Elandon Books, 1981.

McCallie, S. W. *A Preliminary Report on the Marbles of Georgia* [Geological Survey of Georgia Bulletin, 1]. Atlanta: The Franklin Printing and Publishing Co., 1894.

McCornack, W. R., et al. "The Experimental Gallery." *Boston Museum of Fine Arts. Communications to the Trustees.* Privately printed. 4 (1906).

Mead, Edwin D. "The New University at Cleveland." *Education* 3, 1 (September 1882): 1-13.

"A Museum Coming." *The Ohio Architect and Builder* 15, 3 (March 1910): 51.

"A Museum of Photographs." *Architectural Record* 12 (August 1902): 348-350.

"A New Art Museum." *The Ohio Architect and Builder* 7, 6 (June 1906): 41-42.

Nye, Katherine Buell. "The New Cleveland Museum of Art." *Art and Archaeology* 3 (April 1916): 233-235.

Piña, Leslie A. *Louis Rorimer: A Man of Style.* Kent, OH: Kent State University Press, 1990.

"Public Museum Appreciated." *The Ohio Architect and Builder* 22, 1 (July 1913): 62-63.

Ripley, Sidney Dillon. *The Sacred Grove: Essays on Museums.* New York: Simon and Schuster, 1969.

Roberts, Edward A. *Official Report of the Centennial Celebration of the Founding of the City of Cleveland and the Settlement of the Western Reserve.* Cleveland: The Cleveland Printing and Publishing Company, 1896.

Ryder, Albert. "The New Cleveland Museum of Art." *American Magazine of Art* 7, 10 (August 1916): 392-397.

Searing, Helen. *New American Art Museums.* Los Angeles and London: Whitney Museum of American Art in association with the University of California Press, Berkeley, 1982.

Sturgis, R. Clipston. *Report on Plans Presented to the Building Committee.* Privately Printed. Boston: Museum of Fine Arts, 1905.

Townsend, James Benjamin. *100: The Buffalo Fine Arts Academy, 1862-1962.* Buffalo, NY, 1962.

"Training for Museum Work." *Nation* 85, 2194 (July 18, 1907): 50-51.

Viollet-le-Duc, Eugène-Emmanuel. *Discourses on Architecture.* Translated by Benjamin Bucknall. 2 vols. Boston: Ticknor and Co., 1889-1890.

Wagner, Otto. "Modern Architecture." Translated by Nathan Clifford Ricker. *The Brickbuilder* 10 (1901): 124-128, 143-147, 165-171.

Whitehill, Walter Muir. *Museum of Fine Arts Boston, A Centennial History.* 2 vols. Cambridge, MA: Belknap Press, 1970.

Whiting, Frederic Allen. "The Cleveland Museum of Art." *Art and Archaeology* 16, 4-5 (October-November 1923): 186-194.

Wittke, Carl. *The First Fifty Years: The Cleveland Museum of Art.* Cleveland: The John Huntington Art and Polytechnic Trust and The Cleveland Museum of Art, 1966.

Wittlin, Alma. *Museums: In Search of a Usable Future.* Cambridge, MA, and London: M. I. T. Press, 1970.

Wixom, Nancy Coe. *Cleveland Institute of Art, The First Hundred Years.* Cleveland, 1983.

Wood, James M. "The Wades' Grand Tour." *Cleveland Magazine* 14, 6 (June 1985): 98-108.

"The Work of Mr. J. Milton Dyer." *Architectural Record* 20, 5 (November 1905): 384-403.

Wyer, Raymond. "The Cleveland Museum of Art: An Impression." *International Studio (N. Y.)* 60, suppl. (November 1916): xv-xvii.